Stained Glass
Crafting

TO VIOLA and LUCA,
my favorite children

Glass mask made by
Luca when he was six

I THANK
Milvar of Milan, the company that furnished me with the glass I used for the works in this book;
Etneo of Cologno Monzese (MI) for the welding materials;
Forms of Glass of Milan, the studio that kindly lent me some Tiffany objects for the section on ideas;
Chain of Glass and Glassic Art of Milan, who gave me some glassworks for the fused-glass section;
Cristina Grazioli of Rome for the collage objects;
the Zaccaria Glass Art Laboratory in Milan, which created all the other works;
Silvia Damiani for her availability; and
the Photo Studio staff for their collaboration.
A particular thanks goes to Ezio Grazioli, who helped me with inexhaustible patience.

D.Z.

Library of Congress Cataloging-in-Publication Data Available

Photographs by Alberto Bertoldi and Mario Matteucci
Graphics and layout by Paola Masera and Amelia Verga
Translation by Sally Bloomfield

10 9 8 7 6 5 4 3 2 1

Published 1998 by Sterling Publishing Company, Inc.
387 Park Avenue South, New York, N.Y. 10016
Originally published and © 1996 in Italy by R.C.S. Libri & Grandi Opere S.p.A., Milan
under the title *Decorare con il Vetro*
English translation © 1998 by Sterling Publishing Co., Inc.
Distributed in Canada by Sterling Publishing
% Canadian Manda Group, One Atlantic Avenue, Suite 105
Toronto, Ontario, Canada M6K 3E7
Distributed in Great Britain and Europe by Cassell PLC
Wellington House, 125 Strand, London WC2R 0BB, England
Distributed in Australia by Capricorn Link (Australia) Pty Ltd.
P.O. Box 6651, Baulkham Hills, Business Centre, NSW 2153, Australia
Printed in Hong Kong

Sterling ISBN 0-8069-3893-5

Stained Glass Crafting

Donatella Zaccaria

Sterling Publishing Co., Inc.
New York

CONTENTS

INTRODUCTION

"Colored glass offers color to light, and the light brings out the color, transporting it, diffusing it."

In 1979, I began to transform my drawings into glassworks because I was fascinated by glass. I was enchanted by its colors and by the constantly changing effect light had on it. I learned to cut it and to put the pieces together using an ancient method. The results were a translucent mosaic. But my research did not end with this method. I then looked for other materials to use with glass: mother-of-pearl, shells, semiprecious stones, glass mixtures, glass balls, alabaster, and crystals. All these precious materials are translucent. I continued my research, working with glass mosaics and glass fusion. I also worked with antique stained glass, restoring it to its former glory.

I try to create work that evokes different emotions every time light strikes and passes through the glass. Of course, the look changes continuously, depending on the season and the time of day. Light changes during the course of a day and even in the span of a few minutes. I try to be extremely careful in choosing my materials and in projecting them. My "palette" is particularly rich. I try to choose colors that are similar to the transparency of glass mixtures. I only use glass that was made by antique methods. Use the outlines in tin or lead to draw as you would with the lead of a pencil. This is a little secret you need to know in order to understand how to work with stained glass.

WHY USE A MANUAL?

For over twelve years, I've been holding courses in my studio in Milan, teaching the methods of making artistic glasswork. I've met many people: professionals who feel the need to work manually, teachers who want to update their skills with new teaching methods, artists interested in learning other methods, and men and women of all ages. Some of them wanted to change jobs, and some took great pleasure in becoming my competitors. All these people had one thing in common: a passion for glass.

I decided to write this practical manual based on my professional experience, using the same methods I use in my courses.

This book illustrates all the complex stages of working with glass. At the beginning, as you enter the magical world of glass, you may feel overwhelmed. However, with a little practice, you'll gain enough confidence so that glass will become a manageable material, and you will be able to create everything you wish.

I hope to stimulate you and instill a passion for this art which plays with light and color.

Donatella Zaccaria

STAINED GLASS IN HISTORY

THE ORIGINS

The use of glass to create translucent screens enclosed within a window is very old. Known in the Middle East, it was also widespread in Roman and early Christian times.

To support the weight of the roof, the walls of Roman and Byzantine churches had to be extremely solid, with only a few small windows. For this reason, artists decorated the large spaces on the walls with mosaics and frescoes.

In the twelfth century, the Gothic style replaced the Romanesque style. The new architectural style used pillars and supports to hold up the roof. Because the walls no longer had to support this weight, they could have more and bigger windows. These windows were actually panels made with fragments of colored glass held together in a lead frame.

Stained-glass windows quickly replaced mosaics as decorations in churches, and glass artisans developed a style which adapted itself perfectly to glass and lead.

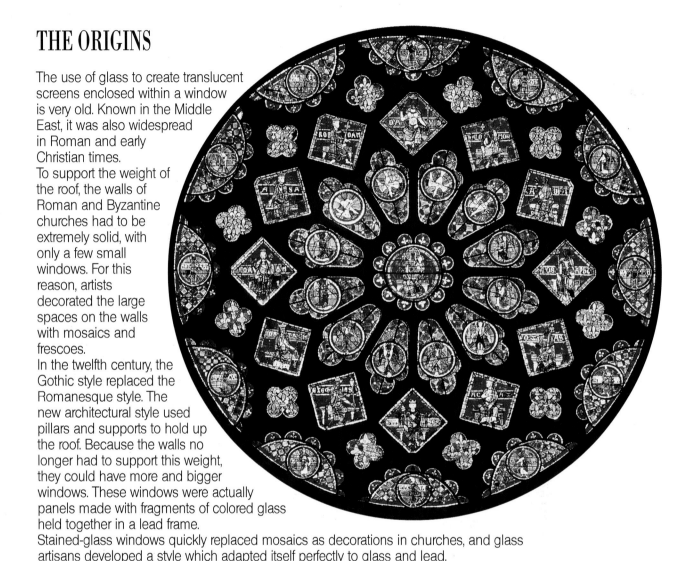

MEDIEVAL TIMES

In medieval times, some windows consisted of glass painted with enamel. The glass was baked at high temperatures to melt the enamel into the glass. Between 1200 and 1236, artisans created the colossal stained glass in the Chartres cathedral. They used about 75,000 square feet (7,000 sq m) of glass. This represents the most important and significant medieval monument to painted glass. In Europe, and particularly in France, this work was of great importance from an artistic point of view. While the art of stained glass came later to Italy, Italian stained glass windows are distinctive because they were designed by painters and not by glass artisans, as was the case in northern Europe.

Chartres cathedral
Glorification of the Virgin
Centerpiece: Madonna with Child
First circle: Four Doves and Angels
Second circle: The Twelve Kings of Judea
Third circle: Prophets

The basilica of Assisi is the most prestigious example of Italian stained glass. Great artists such as Duccio of Buoninsegna, Simone Martini, and Antonio of Pisa painted with a sense of volume and perspective. You can find an excellent example by Buoninsegna (1289) in the Siena cathedral.

In 1300, Antonio of Pisa wrote the first classical piece of literature on Italian glasswork, *Memoirs of Teaching the Making of Glass Windows.* This work is a practical manual by a glass artisan. The author suggests which elements to consider when choosing the colors of the panes of glass to make a window. He teaches how to cut the panes following the desired outline and how to join the glass to the lead. In addition, he describes various techniques to restore windows to their former splendor after bad weather and time have deteriorated them. In this book, he teaches the first secrets of how to create more intricate glasswork, including which colors to use and where to find them. He also teaches the secret of red, silver, yellow, and cobalt blue and indicates what substances to add to molten glass.

Although we aren't certain of exact dates on the origins of painted glass, the use of colored glass joined together to form windows dates back to the first centuries A.D. The oldest fragments are in Ravenna. They come from the fourth century A.D. However, not until the ninth and tenth centuries did stained glass windows reach their full splendor and become more widespread.

The first comprehensive text about the technique of making stained-glass windows is an extract by Teofilo, a German monk who lived in the eleventh century.

CUTTING GLASS

Antonio of Pisa describes various techniques of cutting glass. The first technique involves the use of an incandescent, pointed, iron implement (the same is used for soldering) passed along a chalk outline on a glass pane. The artisan repeats the process many times, wetting the outline to cool the glass until he obtains a clean break. When using thin panes, the artisan only needs to use the point of a hard mineral to score the pane and then to bend the pane until it breaks along the outline. For extremely thick panes, the text suggests using another technique: wrap the outline in thread soaked in sulfur. Set the thread on fire. While the thread is burning, wet the surface of the glass near the thread to induce the break. Then, cut the pieces, following the outline of the lead. Carefully wash, dry, and insert on the drawing to be reproduced. Glue in place and paint. When the artisan finished decorating the glass, he assembled the pieces into the lead, which was a narrow band with a section in the shape of an H that surrounded each piece of glass. This formed a sort of grid in which he set the panes. Once the artisan finished inserting the glass in the lead, he soldered the joints using tin alloy.

In medieval times, the lead bands were made in a press to avoid leakage. During the Renaissance, the technique changed, and the small glass panes were set in the lead bands using putty to fill the spaces between the panes. The lead acted as a setting and a suspension agent. Artisans prepared this putty in various ways, often following a

Louis Comfort Tiffany
Glycine Glasswork
1905
Morse Gallery of Art
Winter Park, Florida

"secret" method. Generally, the putty was composed of one or more organic binding materials, such as oil or powder. The putty was tinted with lampblack.

In the nineteenth century, the art of stained glass experienced a rebirth.

In this period, artisans restored many great works based on Antonio of Pisa's text. Using this text helped many artisans rediscover the old secrets.

This renascence of interest began in France, but by the end of the century Germany had become the center of artistic glasswork in Europe. The use of windows in buildings became more widespread, and often the buildings had nothing to do with religion. Stained glass appeared in the doors, windows, and ceilings of palaces and manor houses. They no longer depicted only sacred themes. Coats of arms, hunting scenes, architectural landscapes, and the first images of common human figures began to appear in glasswork. This change was largely due to the influence of the artistic trends of the era.

Marc Chagall
The Tribe of Levi, detail
Synagogue
of the Hadassah
Hospital, Jerusalem

ART NOUVEAU AND MODERN STYLE

From 1890 to 1930, Art Nouveau, Modern Art, and Art Deco exploded across Europe. These new styles covered all decorative techniques, and stained glassworks had a new moment of glory. The delicate floral and geometric designs of these styles gave life to the production of great new techniques and decorative ideas. Famous artists, designers, and architects, such as Gaudí in Spain, Mackintosh in Scotland, and Grasset in France, created stained glassworks, leaving us splendid evidence of the epoch.

In New York, Louis Comfort Tiffany developed a new technique for assembling pieces of glass. In place of the lead drawing sticks, he used copper leaf covered in tin alloy. He also produced new types of opalescent and iridescent glass.

Tiffany was an excellent painter and had a fondness for nature themes. To reproduce them in his glasswork, he carefully studied the details of plants, flowers, leaves, and animals. Using beautiful glass produced in his own laboratories, he created contrasts between transparency and opalescence so fine that they seem to be real.

Tiffany became famous for his lampshades. Everyone imitated them, but for Tiffany they were not as important as some of his other art. His work represents an excellent union between art and craftsmanship.

In the pictorial field, avant-garde artists have produced works worthy of note. Glass attracted many artists in the twentieth century. The glassworks of Marc Chagall, Henri Matisse, Braque, and Léger are examples of how great artists combined the techniques of stained glass with the techniques of painting to give life to a work of art.

GLASS

GLASS

The origins of glass are cloudy and uncertain. In the opinion of Plinius, the Phoenicians discovered glass rather casually around 5000 B.C. We cannot be sure who were the first people to adopt the art of glassmaking, but ancient Egyptians seem to have played an important role.
From 1500 B.C. on, Egyptians used glass to make objects for personal decoration. Then, they began to create precious works such as the glass case in which the mummy of Ramses II was found.

The method used to make these objects involved setting glass in a press; the ancient Egyptians did not blow glass. However, in 100 A.D., the Romans began to use this method. They would blow glass into a press to make the first panes used in windows.
This method of manufacturing glass panes, still used today, was perfected in medieval times.
The Crusaders brought the secrets of working glass to Venice. The glass industry made the Venetian island of Murano synonymous with the art of glass.
The method of producing flat panes of glass, called "discs," had been in use for centuries at the time of Antonio of Pisa.

USING THE DISC METHOD

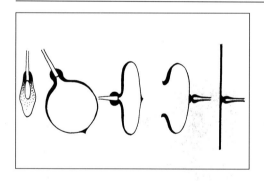

The artisan takes the glass on a straw (1) and blows it into the shape of a sphere (2). Then he squashes it (3) and attaches a prop to the opposite side of the straw (4). At this point, he detaches the straw. He creates the disc by heating and rapidly rotating the sphere. Once the disc cools, the artisan cuts the panes he wants to use to compose his glasswork. Over centuries, artisans slowly perfected this method. In medieval times, it was possible to produce discs with a diameter up to $19\frac{3}{4}$ inches (50 cm).
Later, artisans invented the cylinder method. The advantage of this method was that artisans could produce larger panes of glass.

USING THE CYLINDER METHOD

The artisan takes the necessary quantity of glass on a straw and makes an elongated ball with a diameter of about 12 inches (30 cm). He pulls out the sides of this ball, cuts the cylinder, and then rolls the glass out to produce a pane of glass.

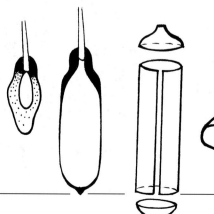

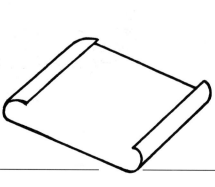

THE CHEMICAL COMPOSITION OF GLASS

Glass is composed of a mixture of silica, soda or potassium, and lime. The artisan adds metal oxides to create various colors. For example, adding iron oxide makes green, selenium or cadmium makes orange and red, and cobalt makes blue. The artisan melts these components together until the result is a boiling liquid. At this stage, he prepares the glass to be blown, spun, and pressed. Then, he cools it. This cooling stage is extremely delicate because the liquid glass must not crystallize while cooling. The right temperature is fundamental when making glass panes for windows, because the artisan must be able to cut the panes without breaking them.

BLOWN GLASS

Artists and artisans still blow glass using ancient methods. Blown glass is noted for its extreme brilliance, an irregular but smooth surface, and internal air bubbles. The color samples are divided into light, medium, and deep, as well as special or plated colors. In different areas, artisans used different techniques to produce the glass. For example, French blown glass is different from English or German. In addition, each factory has its own particular color samples.

NEW ANTIQUE GLASS

This industrial glass, produced in large transparent panes, has a smooth surface noted for its irregular marks which simulate the faults found in glass produced in the old-fashioned way. Compared to blown glass, the color samples are quite limited. This type of glass can be used in glass fusion.

CATHEDRAL GLASS

Antique cathedral glass was known for its marbled, irregular surface and its vast range of colors. Today, industrial cathedral glass is produced in large panes with a regular marbled surface but with limited color samples.

OPALESCENT GLASS

This type of glass is translucent and has a marbled surface. It is made of glass powder mixed in various colors. The famous designer Louis Comfort Tiffany created it. He used it mainly in making lampshades. The range of colors is far richer than the limited color scheme in this piece of glasswork.

WISPY GLASS

This glass is opalescent but more transparent, with raised opaque *traces on the surface. These create an effect of depth.* *Iridescent glasswork is obtained by oxidizing the smoother side of* *opalescent and wispy glass. It has a rich mother-of-pearl effect.*

TOOLS USED FOR CUTTING GLASS

In times past, the experts used red-hot iron tools or precious stones such as diamonds or zirconium. Today, various types of special stainless-steel rolling cutters are available.

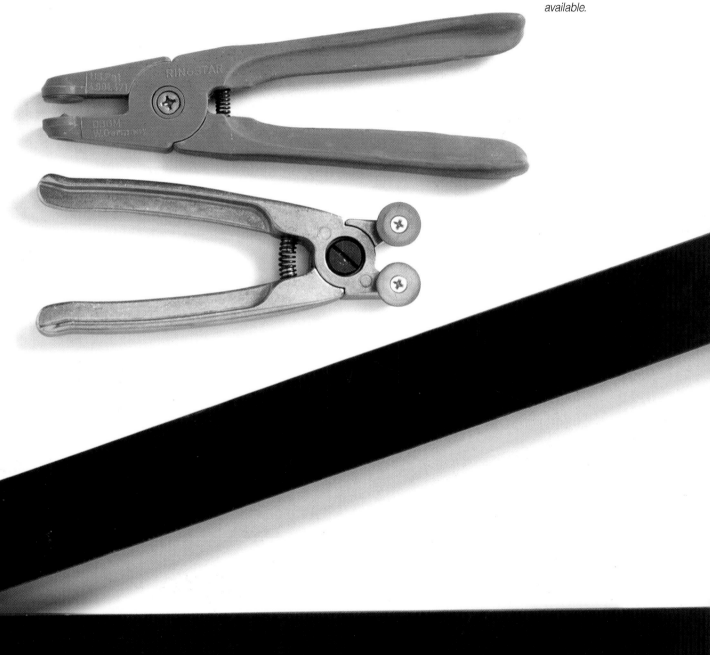

You can find several types of glass cutters: normal scissors and scissors with three blades that cut the double line of the cardboard. Pliers include those used to open the cuts and to finish the glass (for beginners normal pliers with limited teeth are sufficient). You can also buy a set-square to cut the glass panes.

CUTTING THE GLASS

STRAIGHT CUTS

- First, score the glass. Find the most comfortable way to grip the glass cutter and run the cutter from the beginning to the very end of the glass you want to cut. Scoring produces a sound similar to hissing. You should see a continuous white line on the glass. Never go over the score. In the beginning, practice by cutting normal window glass until you have mastered the technique. Then, continue with cathedral glass, scoring the smooth side and applying force while cutting.

- To break a scored piece of glass, hold the glass with two hands on either side of the score. Apply equal force on both sides. Be careful not to let the glass slip.

- If you have scored the glass correctly, the glass will snap easily. You must practice scoring and breaking a lot of glass without worrying about wasting it. You'll need a great deal of practice to gain confidence in your ability to perform this operation.

- After you have scored and broken the piece by hand, score it again, many times. Always remember to score from the beginning to the very end of the piece. The second time, try to snap the glass with the pliers.

- Position the pliers so that they are parallel to and close to the score. Use your other hand to hold the glass firmly. With the pliers on one side and your hand on the other, press again, and the glass should snap.

- Repeat this exercise until you feel confident. Pay attention to the pieces of glass that shatter and always hold the glass away from your face.

CUTTING USING A CARDBOARD TEMPLATE

Now, choose the shape you wish to make.
- Take a piece of cardboard and draw a square with $1\frac{1}{4}$-inch (3 cm) sides. This will be your template. Cut it out of the cardboard and position it on the glass, holding it firmly with your hand.
- Try to score the glass with your glass cutter, following the edge of the template. Score all four sides. The scoring must go to the very end of the glass. If the cardboard moves, position it again. Have several cardboard squares ready. In the beginning, you may find it difficult to follow the edge perfectly, and the resulting pieces of glass will probably be bigger than your original cardboard template. Have patience and keep trying.

- After scoring the square on the glass, break off the biggest pieces by hand.

- Use the pliers to break off the pieces of glass nearest the score. You should have a piece of glass identical to your original cardboard square. Check this. If the glass square is bigger than your original, try again.
- Use a cardboard template only twice and then use a new one. Make other templates in geometrical shapes such as rectangles and triangles, and practice cutting them out in glass.

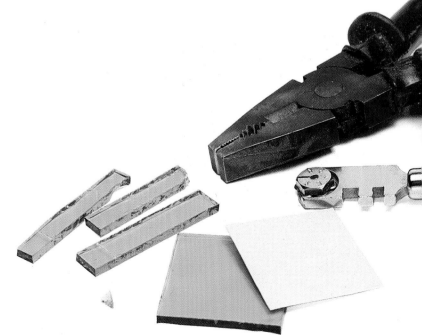

CUTTING CURVED OR SHAPED GLASS PIECES

Cutting curves is more complex.
- Make templates by drawing shapes with concave or convex lines. Score them on your glass, making sure that the scoring always goes to the very end of the piece of glass.
- After you use the template to score, you must score other lines that follow the shape you want to create. Now, you are ready to begin cutting.

- Using pliers, break off the outside pieces. Break off the biggest pieces until you are near the shape you scored. You'll have a lot of glass chips. Break them off one at a time and keep your worktable clear.

Some cuts break off in one piece; however, for others you'll need to chip away at the glass. To get a perfectly smooth edge, use a grinding wheel. This will help you remove all the pieces which didn't break off cleanly. Check again to be sure that the resulting piece of glass is identical to your template. Repeat the process with another pane of glass.

CUTTING A LEAF

- Make a leaf-shaped cardboard template and score it on your glass, remembering to hold it firmly.
- Score straight lines around the leaf shape.
- Using pliers, break off the outside pieces of glass until you are left with the desired leaf shape.
- Check that the leaf-shaped glass is identical to your original template.

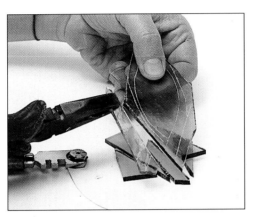
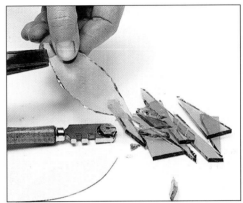

CUTTING POINTED SHAPES

- As always, practice with easy shapes until you feel confident enough go on to more difficult ones. After working with cathedral glass, try cutting opalescent glass — which is always cut on the smooth side. This glass requires more force when scoring.

THE TIFFANY METHOD

This method, invented at the end of nineteenth century by Louis Comfort Tiffany, is the least complicated method using lead. Thus, it is especially suitable for beginners.

Many glass artists use the Tiffany method because it works so well when the artist has many small pieces of glass that would be difficult to solder using the more gridlike lead technique. This method is also suitable for curved work, such as lampshades. Some glass artists mix the two methods.

TOOLS AND MATERIALS FOR WELDING

COPPER WIRE

Artists use copper wire in the shape of a C to go around the various pieces of glass which make up parts of glasswork. The inner side of the wire is adhesive and is available in several widths. You can use copper ribbon manually or with a feeder made for this purpose.

The electric grinder allows you to finish off the glass pieces so that they have perfectly smooth edges. It is easy to use and is especially useful when you are cutting curves and working with pliers.

WELDERS

Various types of welders with different heat strengths and with different copper heads are available on the market. They will melt the solder. The flux keeps the solder liquefied. It makes welding easier and prevents the copper heads from oxidizing. It is painted on with a paintbrush.

PLANNING YOUR GLASSWORK

To create artistic glasswork, you begin by drawing a detailed plan. When studying your sketches, consider the glass and only keep a design which allows you to cut the pieces properly. During the preparatory phase, make a small-scale version of your drawing and try various color possibilities in order to visualize the final effect. Use a scale of 1:1 and copy the design on a piece of tracing paper. To make a Tiffany design, remember to draw narrow double lines between the connecting glass pieces. If you are using the lead method, draw the double lines about the width of the lead wire.

To enlarge your design to the dimensions you want, use a projector or a photocopier. Make a copy on cardboard and a copy on regular paper. Cut out the cardboard design so that you have cardboard templates for scoring.

Use the paper drawing to check that your glass pieces are the right size for welding. You may find that carbon paper is helpful when you want to make copies without a photocopier. Choosing your colors is very important. They will look different on paper than they will in glass. Look at the glass on a light box or against a light to see what the effect will be.

STRAIGHT EDGED GLASSWORK

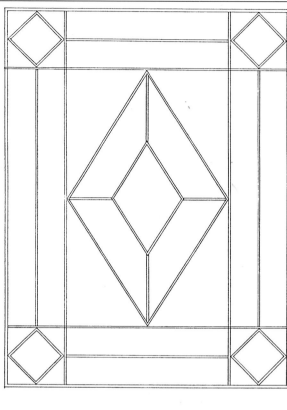

EQUIPMENT

- **5 sheets of 9 3/4 x 9 3/4 inch (25 x 25 cm) cathedral glass in different colors**
- **glass cutter**
- **pliers**
- **scissors**
- **50/50 solder**
- **copper ribbon**
- **flux**
- **welder**

- Enlarge this design using a photocopier and make copies on paper and on cardboard.

- Use cathedral glass. Choose your colors. Now, you are ready to begin.

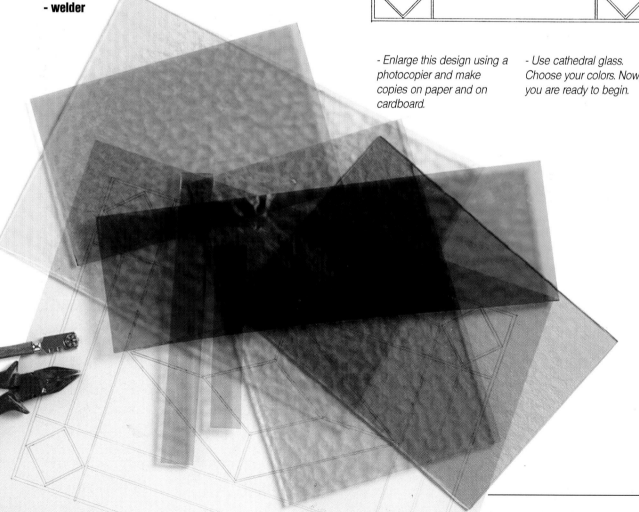

CUTTING THE GLASS

Use the cardboard templates to score the glass.
Place the pieces of glass on the paper copy.
- Cut out the templates. Remember to eliminate the double line you drew.
- Begin using the square template and green glass.

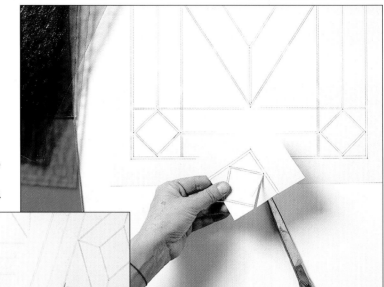

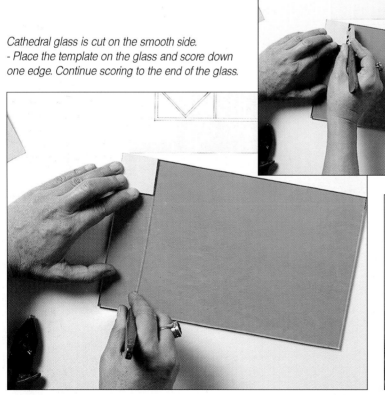

Cathedral glass is cut on the smooth side.
- Place the template on the glass and score down one edge. Continue scoring to the end of the glass.

- To break off this rectangle, tap under the pane at the beginning of the score. The glass should break easily.

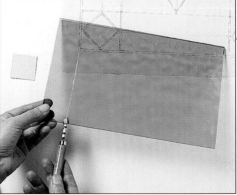

- Hold the glass on either side of the score.
- Snap off the rectangle using equal force on both sides.

- Place the template onto the glass rectangle again and score the last side.
- Break the glass square off and place it on the paper copy. Check that it is identical to the design. If it isn't, start again and make a new square.

- Continue cutting all the pieces, first making the template and then cutting the glass and placing it on the paper copy. Use the turquoise glass for the central rhombus and the small triangles.

- Where you can, break off the pieces by hand. Where necessary, use pliers. Keep your worktable clean and eliminate any glass chips with a brush. Now you will be able to visualize this piece with the different colors.

*- Continue using the
yellow and pink glass.*

*- Here, all the pieces
have been cut.
Remember to check
every piece carefully to
make sure it
corresponds to the
original design. If one
piece isn't perfect, do it
again.*

TRIMMING

EQUIPMENT

- **copper ribbon**
- **scissors**
- **cutter**
- **glass cutter**

Originally, preglued copper ribbons were not available in the Tiffany studio. Artisans trimmed glass by cutting and folding strips of copper to form a C-shape. In order to attach the strips to the glass, they filled the C-shaped strips with beeswax!
- Before you proceed to the second phase of your work, clean the table of all glass chips. Remove the sheets of glass you used and put away the copper ribbon, the scissors, the cutter, and the glass cutter.
- Decide the width of ribbon you are going to use. Before you start trimming, wash your hands and clean the glass pieces with a dry towel.

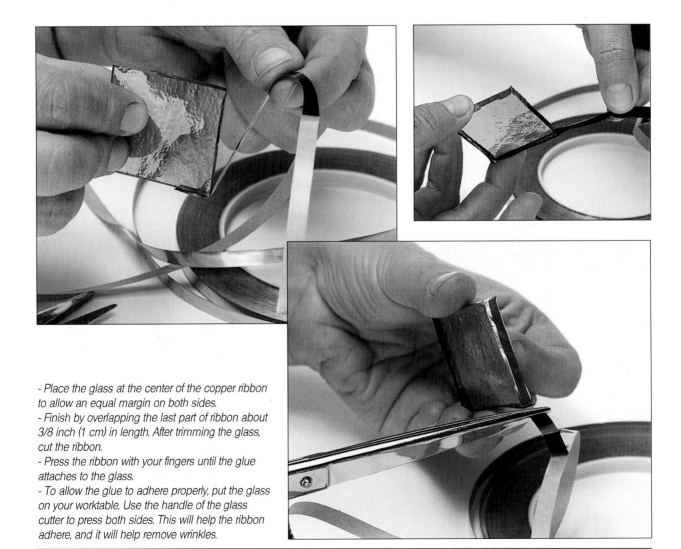

- Place the glass at the center of the copper ribbon to allow an equal margin on both sides.
- Finish by overlapping the last part of ribbon about 3/8 inch (1 cm) in length. After trimming the glass, cut the ribbon.
- Press the ribbon with your fingers until the glue attaches to the glass.
- To allow the glue to adhere properly, put the glass on your worktable. Use the handle of the glass cutter to press both sides. This will help the ribbon adhere, and it will help remove wrinkles.

- Press the ribbon in with your fingers to form a C-shape surrounding the glass edges.
- Remove all imperfections, using the cutter.

- Proceed from one piece to the other.
- If the ribbon is not straight, remove it and repeat the process. To a great extent, the final result depends on how evenly you trim.

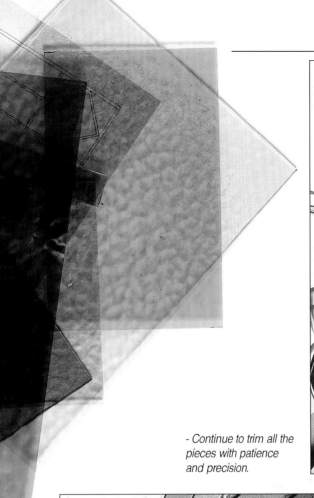

- Continue to trim all the pieces with patience and precision.

- The ribbon should form a straight and continuous line. Where there are imperfections, unfold the copper using the cutter to straighten the line.

- Be sure to press hard on the ribbon in order to permit the glue to stick properly. Check that you have trimmed all the glass pieces properly and lay them on the paper.

- Once you have finished trimming all the pieces, you can begin the welding process.

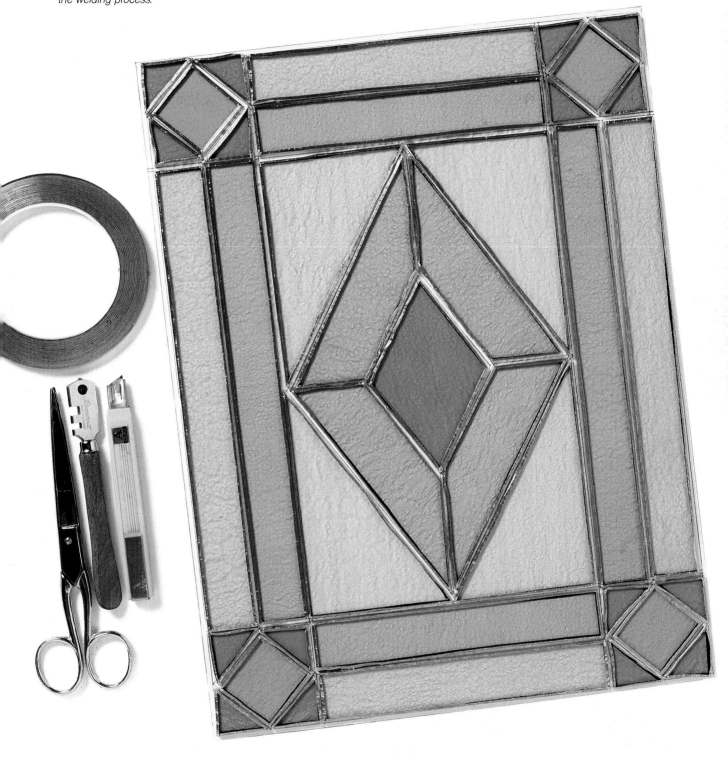

WELDING

In order to weld this first piece, you should have a wooden worktable, a brick on which you can place the welder, 50/50 solder, flux, and a paintbrush to spread the flux. The flux helps the solder stick to the copper and makes the solder more fluid and flexible.

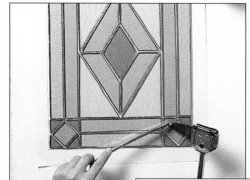

- First, fix the glass pieces to avoid any movement.
- Begin with the outer pieces. Dip the brush in the flux and brush the copper ribbon.

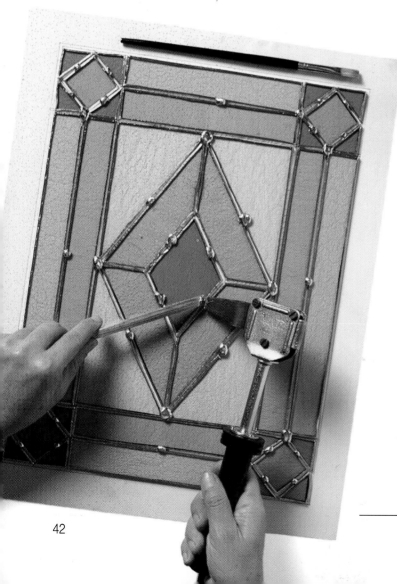

- Plug in the welder. When it reaches the right temperature, the solder will melt.
- Put the solder on the head of the welder and bring it near the glass in the spots where you have applied the flux.
- Melt a drop of solder to attach one piece of glass to another.
- Continue to melt drops of solder on all the peripheral pieces to fix them to each other. Don't be afraid to touch the glass with the welder; glass resists heat.
- Continue until you have attached all the peripheral pieces.
- At this point, attach the central pieces with welding drops. Remember to wet the copper with the flux.

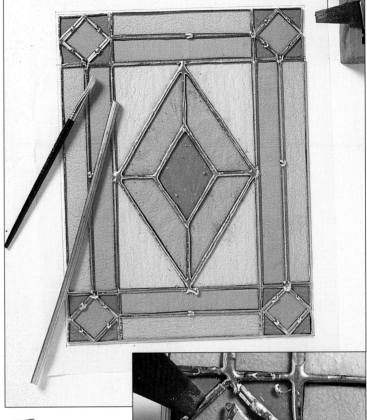

- Once you have trimmed all the pieces of glass and put them in place, begin the real welding. First, apply the flux to the copper ribbon, beginning with the central rhombus. Cut off 3/8 inch (1 cm) of solder.

- Touch the head of the welder to the copper ribbon. Wait until the solder begins to melt. When it becomes fluid, pull the piece, following the line of the copper ribbon.

- Separate another piece of solder, heat it and pull it, continuing to cover the copper. In order to create smooth joints, all you have to do is apply the heat of the welder to the point and let the solder distribute evenly.

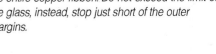

- Weld the entire central part without skipping from one point to another of the figure.

- Start at one point and continue, joining all the fixed points you created before.

- Before welding a piece, always remember to apply the flux. If you have forgotten, you will immediately notice that the solder does not cover the copper as easily and evenly.

- When you have finished the central part, continue with the outer pieces. Each time a strip meets another, stop and repeat the process in order to connect two separate pieces of welding.

- The welding should bulge a little so that it covers the entire copper ribbon. Do not exceed the limit of the glass, instead, stop just short of the outer margins.

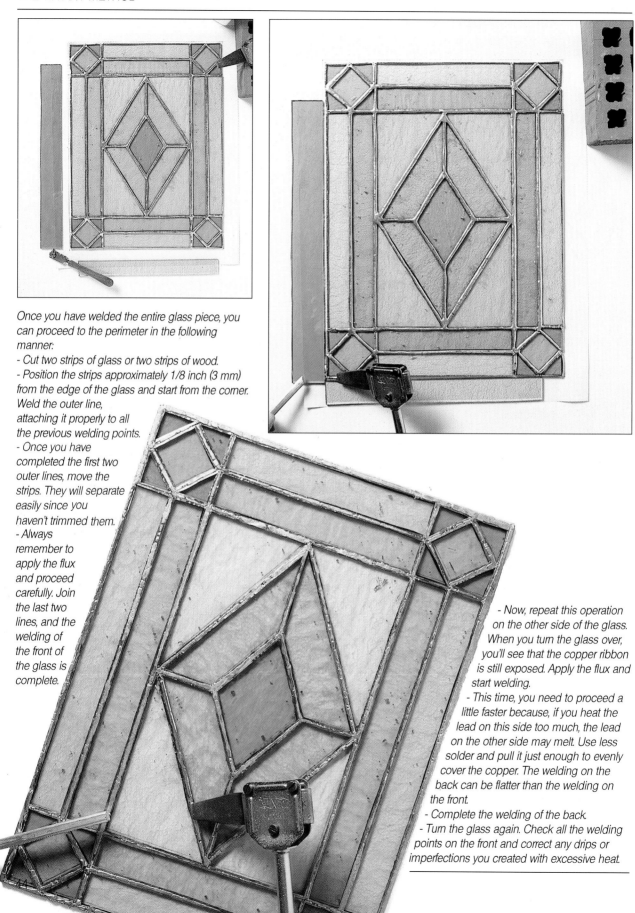

Once you have welded the entire glass piece, you can proceed to the perimeter in the following manner:
- Cut two strips of glass or two strips of wood.
- Position the strips approximately 1/8 inch (3 mm) from the edge of the glass and start from the corner. Weld the outer line, attaching it properly to all the previous welding points.
- Once you have completed the first two outer lines, move the strips. They will separate easily since you haven't trimmed them.
- Always remember to apply the flux and proceed carefully. Join the last two lines, and the welding of the front of the glass is complete.

- Now, repeat this operation on the other side of the glass. When you turn the glass over, you'll see that the copper ribbon is still exposed. Apply the flux and start welding.
- This time, you need to proceed a little faster because, if you heat the lead on this side too much, the lead on the other side may melt. Use less solder and pull it just enough to evenly cover the copper. The welding on the back can be flatter than the welding on the front.
- Complete the welding of the back.
- Turn the glass again. Check all the welding points on the front and correct any drips or imperfections you created with excessive heat.

- Wash the glass with a wet cloth and soapy water.
- Remove all traces of the welding and any drops of solder.

CURVED CUTTING FOR AN OVAL PIECE

EQUIPMENT

- 7 sheets of opalescent glass 12 x 12 inches (30 x 30 cm) each
- glass cutter
- pliers
- scissors
- 50/50 solder
- copper ribbon
- flux
- welder

- Enlarge this design on a photocopier to make a paper copy and a cardboard template. If you can't use a photocopier, use carbon paper.

- Use color reproductions to help choose the colors you want to use.
- Choose glass sheets that resemble the colors you have chosen.
- For this second exercise, use opalescent glass. This is harder to cut, but it offers more interesting colors, and the results will be rewarding.

CUTTING

- Begin cutting out the design for the pieces at the bottom of the design. Cut the cardboard and remove the double line.
- Use an opalescent light blue glass with blue veins. Cut this type of glass on its smooth side. The surface of the opalescent glass is not as uniform as that of cathedral glass, and it is more difficult to cut.

- Score the glass. Since this design contains only curved lines, you will have to use the cutter. Remember to approach the cutting line with multiple cuttings in the same direction. Keep the table clean, removing all glass chips with a brush.
- Once you have cut the first piece, check that it matches the card template and place it on the paper model.

- Continue with the other pieces of the base until you complete it. Then proceed to another color.
- For the leaves and stalks, use different types of green glass to obtain different color effects and tones.

- Cut the flowers from white opalescent glass and some pieces of pink glass. Cut out the cardboard template and score the glass, approaching the cutting line with multiple cuts in the same direction to gradually obtain the right shape. Small pieces are not easy to cut because they are hard to hold.
- Use opalescent yellow glass for the pistils.

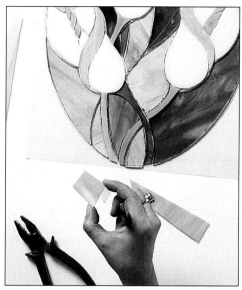

TRIMMING

Trimming curved glass is no harder than trimming straight forms with angles.
- Clean the glass pieces before you begin trimming.
- Position the first piece at the center of the ribbon. Be careful not to leave spaces on the curved surfaces.
- Press down with your fingers.

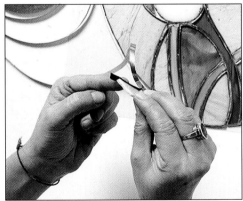

- Curved glass tends to create more wrinkles, so be sure to press the pieces firmly with the handle of the glass cutter. The smaller pieces require greater attention, but with a bit of patience you will be able to trim them successfully.

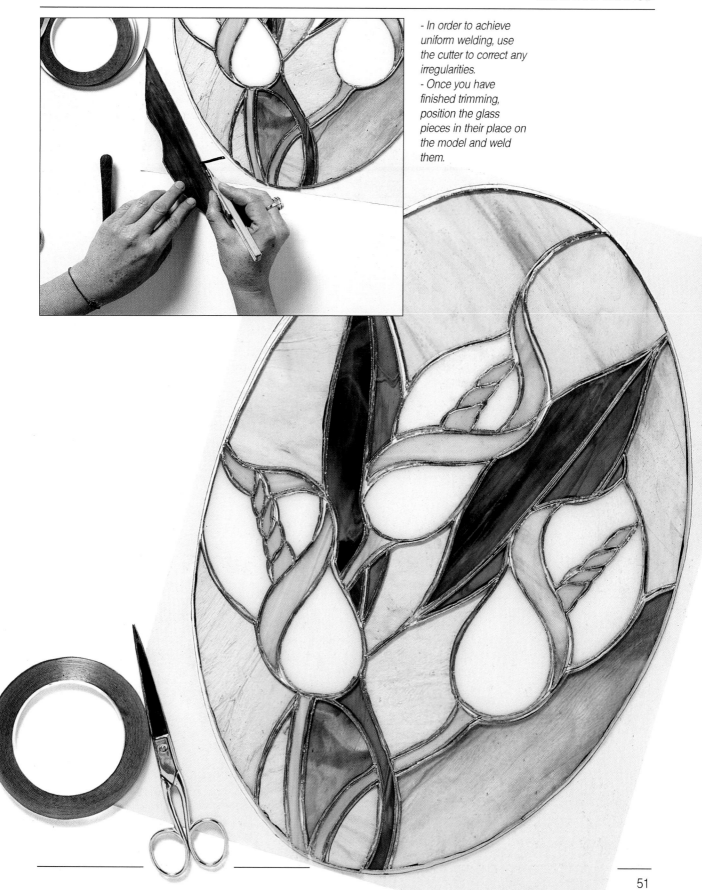

- In order to achieve uniform welding, use the cutter to correct any irregularities.
- Once you have finished trimming, position the glass pieces in their place on the model and weld them.

WELDING

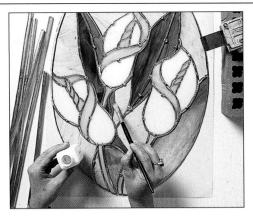

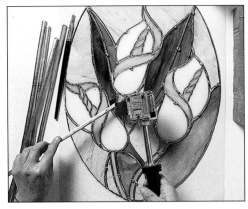

- After you have wet the copper with the flux, fix the different pieces of glass in position to keep them in the proper place.

- Begin the welding. Apply the flux with the brush, cut solder, heat it, and pull it to cover the copper ribbon.
- Continue connecting the different lines of welding.

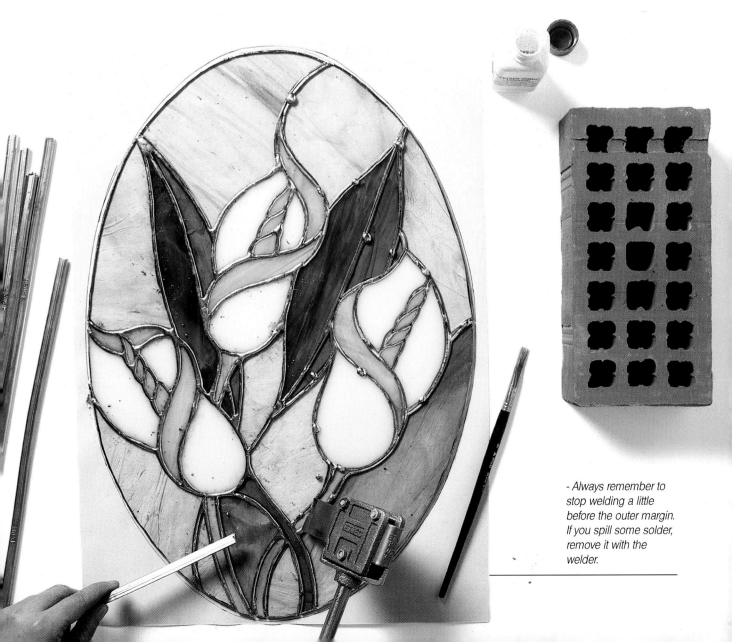

- Always remember to stop welding a little before the outer margin. If you spill some solder, remove it with the welder.

- In order to weld the outer edges, use another piece of glass. Place it on top of the piece of glasswork and draw the curve of the oval on it with a felt-tipped pen. Score the glass along this line.
- Separate the glass with pliers to create a perfect border for your oval. Repeat this process to reproduce any kind of border you may require.
- Place the glass you have created at a distance of approximately 1/8 inch (3 mm) from the oval and begin welding the border.

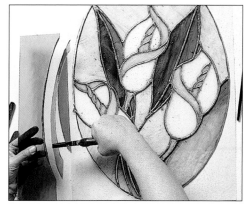

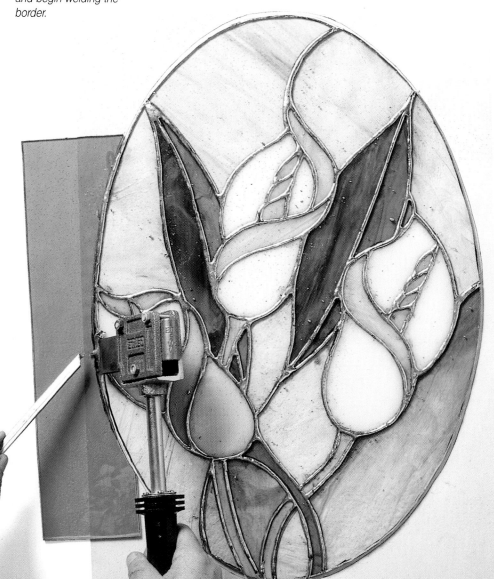

- Whenever necessary, cut additional glass, reproducing the exact curves of the border of the oval. At this point, you have almost finished welding the front.

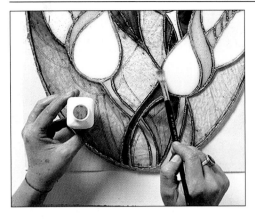

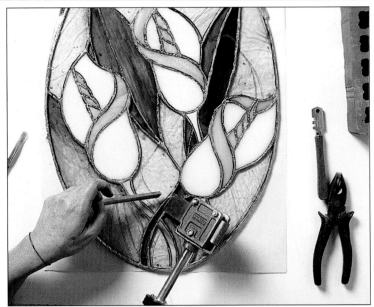

- Turn the piece over and repeat the procedure on the back. Apply the flux and weld. Remember to proceed a bit more quickly to avoid melting the solder on the front.
- Complete the welding on the back and turn the piece over once more.

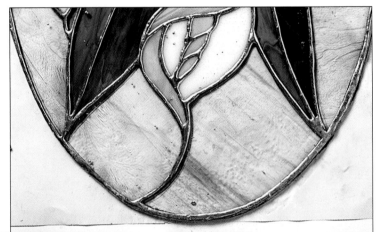

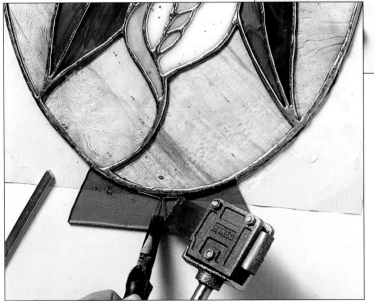

- If you want to hang the oval, for example on a window, prepare a ring with a string of metal and weld it to the border of the oval using some drops of solder.

- Check that all the welding points are uniform and use the welder to correct those that are not. Clean the piece with a cloth and soapy water.
- Use a soft metal file to remove any imperfections on the border.

Place the piece on the worktable, as seen on the right. Hold it gently with your fingers and use a file to finish it off.

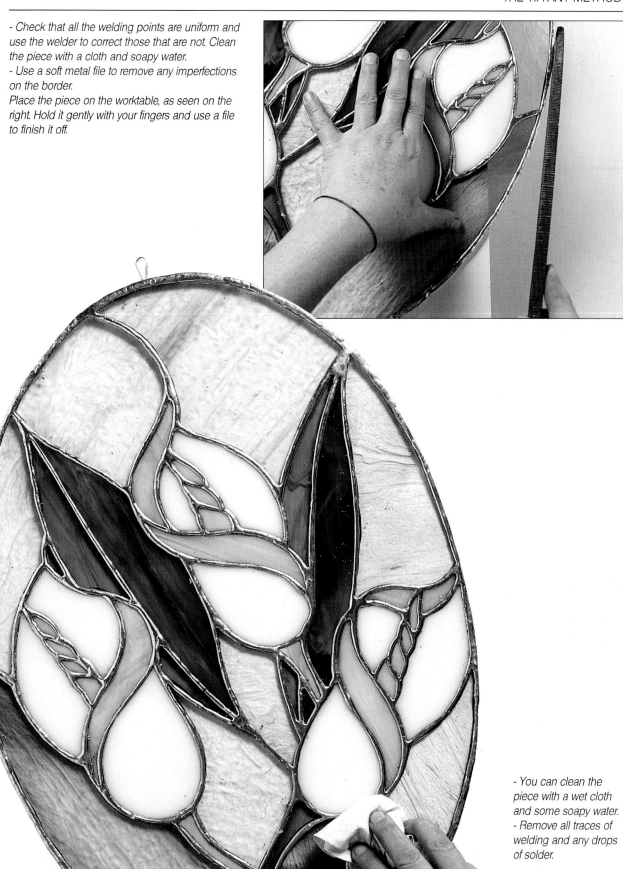

- You can clean the piece with a wet cloth and some soapy water.
- Remove all traces of welding and any drops of solder.

A BOX

EQUIPMENT

- 6 x 6 inch (15 x 15 cm) sheets of mirror glass (for the bottom)
- 6 x 6 inch (15 x 15 cm) sheets of yellow glass (for the sides)
- one 8 x 8 inch (20 x 20 cm) sheet of transparent blown glass (for the sides and the cover)
- four 6 x 6 inch (15 x 15 cm) sheets of different yellow tones (for the butterfly's wings)
- gray glass for the body
- glass cutter
- pliers
- 50/50 solder
- copper ribbon
- flux
- welder
- masking tape

- *Enlarge this drawing to create the paper design from which you will work.*

- *If you wish to use glass in other colors, try them out on your paper copy first.*

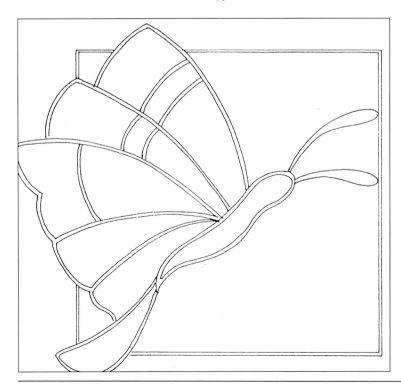

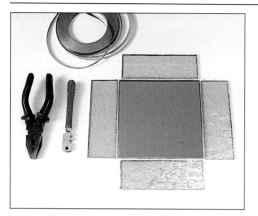

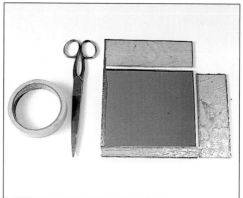

- Cut a square of mirror glass, 6 x 6 inches (15 x 15 cm). Cut the four side pieces of yellow glass in the following manner: two strips 6 inches (15 cm) long and 2 inches (5 cm) wide and two strips 5 5/8 inches (14.5 cm) long and 2 inches (5 cm) wide.
- Trim all the pieces with copper ribbon. Join the sides together with the masking tape and place them on the mirror.

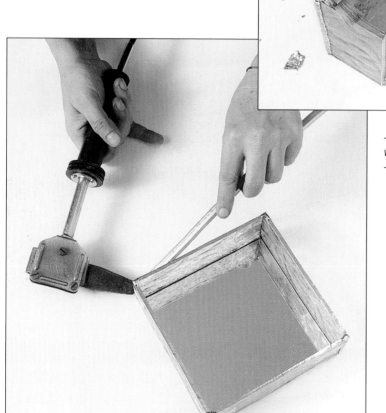

- Wet with the flux and fix the four sides with welding points.
- Join the bottom and the sides with welding points.

- Once you have attached all the pieces, turn the
box on its side, apply the flux, and weld the mirror
bottom and the sides.

- Weld all four sides.
- Turn again and weld the corners.
- After you have welded the sides, weld
from the top to the bottom towards the
mirror glass, where you finish the
welding.

- The dimensions of the finished cover are 6 5/16 x 6 5/16 inches (16 x 16 cm). The cover must be bigger than the base so that it will fit when the box is closed. After you draw the cover design (in this case, a butterfly), cut all the glass pieces, trim them, and weld them. Next, cut the sides of the cover: two pieces 6 5/16 inches (16 cm) long and 3/4 inch (2 cm) wide and two pieces 6 inches (15 cm) long and 3/4 inch (2 cm) wide. Weld the sides to the cover the same way you welded the sides to the base.

61

A TIFFANY LAMPSHADE

EQUIPMENT

- 5 sheets of opalescent glass (red, white, off-white, beige, black) 8 x 8 inches (20 x 20 cm) each
- glass cutter
- pliers
- 50/50 solder
- copper ribbon
- flux
- welder
- brass rosette
- masking tape

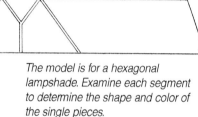

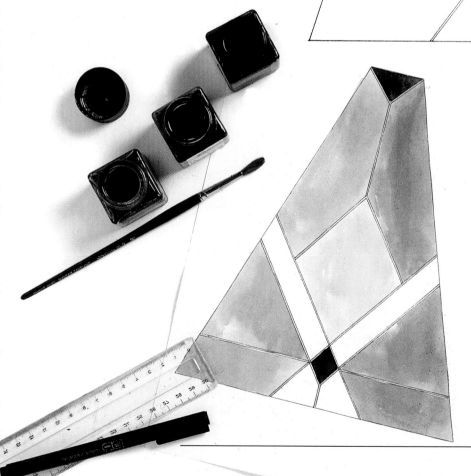

The model is for a hexagonal lampshade. Examine each segment to determine the shape and color of the single pieces.
- Choose the types of glass to combine. Keep in mind that the opalescent types are preferable for lampshades because they hide the electrical apparatus.
- Use this model of a segment. Enlarge it using a photocopier. You'll need six paper copies and six cardboard templates of the piece.

- Begin cutting the glass pieces and put together the first segment of the lampshade.
- Cut all six sides, paying attention to the cutting process. Start cutting one color at a time.

- Trim all the pieces.

- The six segments which form the lampshade will have to match perfectly. Therefore, you must cut and trim each piece precisely. To a large extent, the final result will depend on the way you execute this phase.

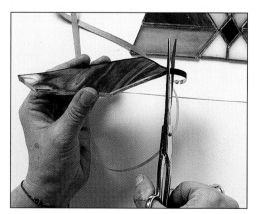

Before you start welding, nail strips of wood to your worktable and make a frame for one segment. Place the different pieces of glass inside the wooden frame. In this way, all six segments will have exactly the same angles.
- Apply the flux and fix the different pieces with welding points.
- Weld the first segment.

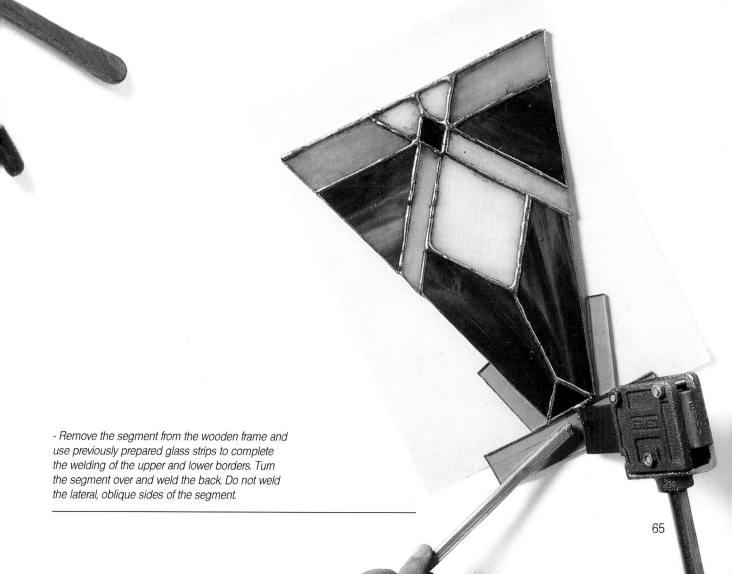

- Remove the segment from the wooden frame and use previously prepared glass strips to complete the welding of the upper and lower borders. Turn the segment over and weld the back. Do not weld the lateral, oblique sides of the segment.

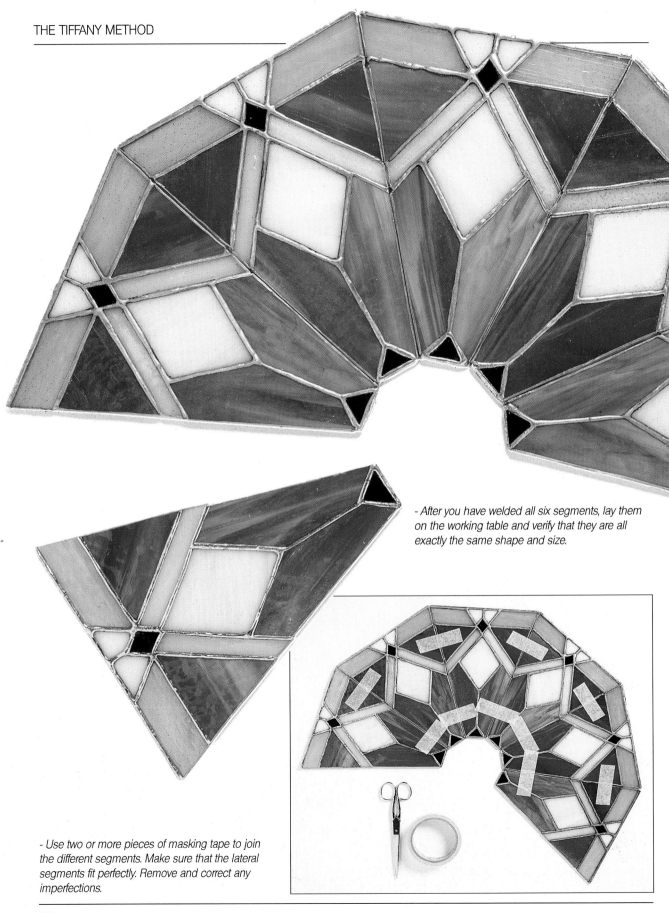

- After you have welded all six segments, lay them on the working table and verify that they are all exactly the same shape and size.

- Use two or more pieces of masking tape to join the different segments. Make sure that the lateral segments fit perfectly. Remove and correct any imperfections.

- *Divide the lampshade into two parts. Lift three segments facing one side of the table and arrange the other pieces opposite the first three.*
- *Use more masking tape to fix all the pieces together to create the final shape of the lampshade.*

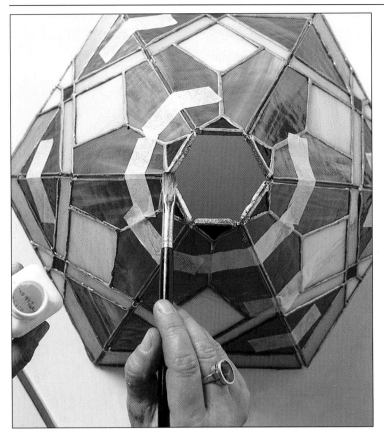

- Apply the flux to the joints. Because only the tape is holding the lampshade together at this point, you should complete this phase quickly to avoid melting the tin.
- Fix the upper edge with welding points. Now the upper part of the lampshade is fixed.

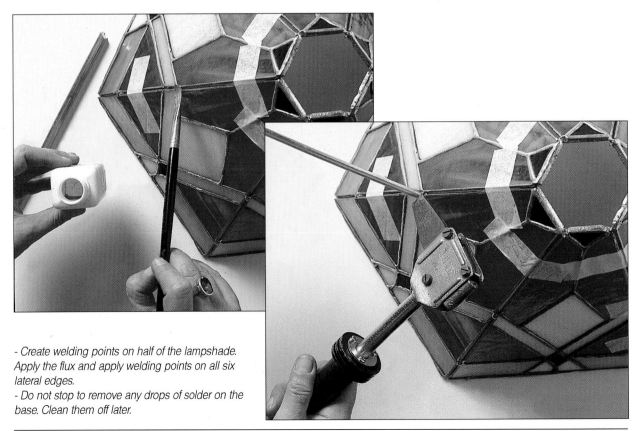

- Create welding points on half of the lampshade. Apply the flux and apply welding points on all six lateral edges.
- Do not stop to remove any drops of solder on the base. Clean them off later.

- Continue adhering the lower border with additional welding points. At this point, you have firmly joined all six segments.
- Turn the lampshade delicately and lay it on the table. Cover the internal lines, attaching two segments together with masking tape.
- Press the tape until it is evenly attached. These strips will prevent the solder from dripping inside the lampshade as you weld.

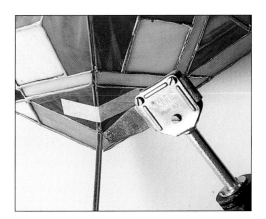

- Turn the lampshade once again and begin to weld. Be sure to have a brick to place the lamp on, so that you will be able to follow the lines that are parallel to your worktable.
- Apply the flux.
- Weld along the lines of the lateral edges that join the two segments. Proceed slowly. Pay attention so that the solder does not drip along the oblique sides. The tape on the inside will prevent the solder from dripping onto the lampshade. Continue until you have welded all six segments.

- Turn the lampshade over and remove the tape. To work more comfortably, place the lampshade inside a cardboard box full of newspapers. Connect the welding line created on the outer surface with the different lines which compose the design of the segments.
- Carefully join the upper borders, using the welder lightly to keep the welding lines straight.
- Now you have finished welding the lampshade. Use your file to finish off all imperfections on the upper border.
- Repeat the process on the lower border.
- Wash the lampshade with a cloth and soapy water and remove all traces of solder from the piece.

- Take a brass rosette with the exact same dimensions as the hole in the top of the lampshade. Once you have welded the rosette to the lampshade, you will be able to hang it or block it at the base.
- Join the rosette to the lamp and wet it with the flux.
- Weld the rosette to all the upper borders of the lampshade, on the inside and the outside.
- If you want a darker-tone weld, you can buy specific products called "patinas."
- Distribute the patina evenly with a brush on the welding. The welding will turn black immediately. Wait a few minutes and wash the lamp.
- You have completed the Tiffany lamp. Mount it on your base and fix it with a screw.

THE LEAD TECHNIQUE

To create glasswork with this technique, begin by making two copies of your design, one on paper and one on cardboard. Draw the double lines for the lead strips the thickness of the lead wire. Cut out all the glass pieces and put them on the paper copy of your design, making certain that they are the right size. With the wooden band in place, put the design on your worktable. The lead wire will substitute for the copper ribbon used earlier in the book. The glass edges should fit into the grooves of the lead. Start working from one corner with the wooden frame at a 90° angle. Adhere the lead to the glass pieces and keep your work in place with nails hammered into the frame. Continue putting the pieces on, one after another. Join the glass and the lead by melting a little lead where the lead trim meets. Turn your work over and solder on the other side, too. The last step is sealing your piece to make it durable. You do this by adding putty between the glass and the lead.

TOOLS AND MATERIALS

LEAD

Lead wire is sold in strips of varying widths. The thickness you use depends on the dimensions of the work and on the size of the glass pieces. The kind of wire used most often is C-shaped. You thread the glass into the grooves of the H until it touches the center of the lead wire. Standard groove edges are usually flat on both sides of the wire, but rounded groove edges are available. You can also find U-shaped wires for outside borders.

The lead wire tends to lose its form in storage, and you must stretch it back into shape. Insert one end of the lead wire into a nautical clamp. Hold the other end with pliers. Pull slowly and avoid unnecessary tugs that could break the lead. If the lead grooves are squashed, you can reshape them with a flat piece of wood. Cut the lead with a knife or a straight spatula used as a cutter.

Welder with thermostat

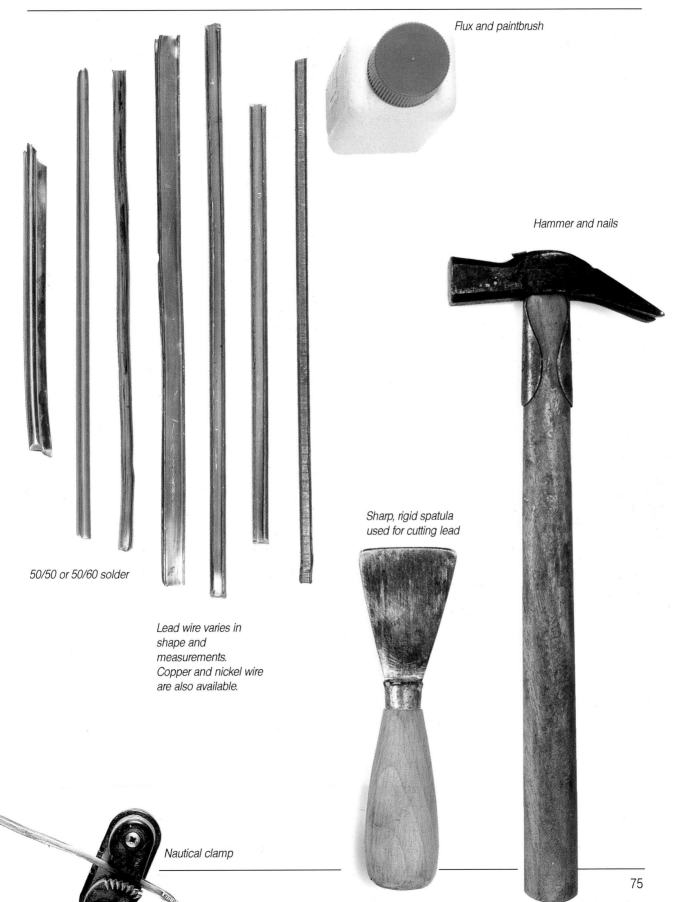

Flux and paintbrush

Hammer and nails

Sharp, rigid spatula
used for cutting lead

50/50 or 50/60 solder

Lead wire varies in
shape and
measurements.
Copper and nickel wire
are also available.

Nautical clamp

75

MULTICOLORED GLASS PANEL

EQUIPMENT

- blown glass in blue, yellow, pink, orange,
  and dark green
- glass cutter
- pliers
- scissors
- lead wire in C-shape or H-shape
- 50/50 solder
- flux
- welder

- Photocopy the picture here and enlarge it to the dimensions you want. Copy the design onto tracing paper and make two copies, one on regular paper and one on cardboard.
- Copy the designs on a 1:1 scale, using the lead technique. Leave space between the glass pieces according to the thickness of the lead.
- Study the position of the colors by making various combinations on the paper copy of your design.

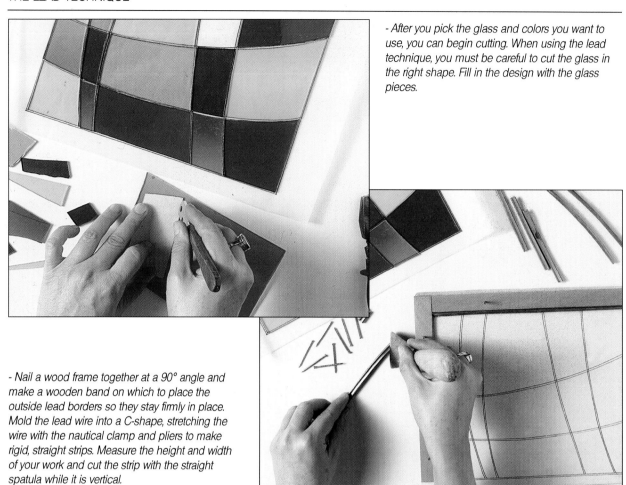

- After you pick the glass and colors you want to use, you can begin cutting. When using the lead technique, you must be careful to cut the glass in the right shape. Fill in the design with the glass pieces.

- Nail a wood frame together at a 90° angle and make a wooden band on which to place the outside lead borders so they stay firmly in place. Mold the lead wire into a C-shape, stretching the wire with the nautical clamp and pliers to make rigid, straight strips. Measure the height and width of your work and cut the strip with the straight spatula while it is vertical.

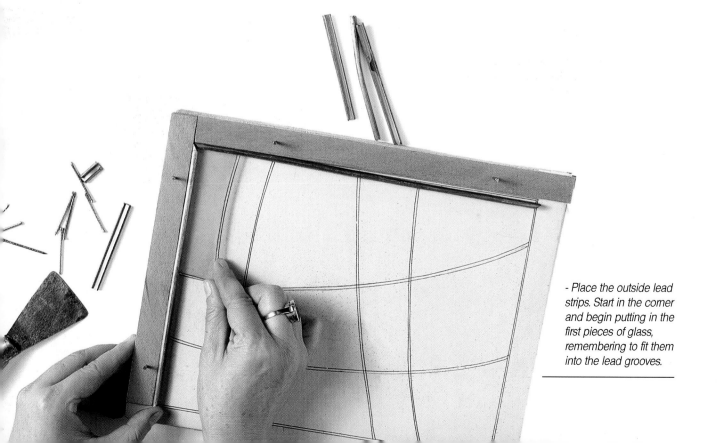

- Place the outside lead strips. Start in the corner and begin putting in the first pieces of glass, remembering to fit them into the lead grooves.

- For the internal part of your piece, use H-shaped lead strips. Measure the longer side of the first glass piece and cut your lead strip accordingly. Insert the glass into the lead strip and keep the lead in place with nails.
- To fix the short side of the glass without using nails too near the glass, use a little piece of lead, as shown here (right).

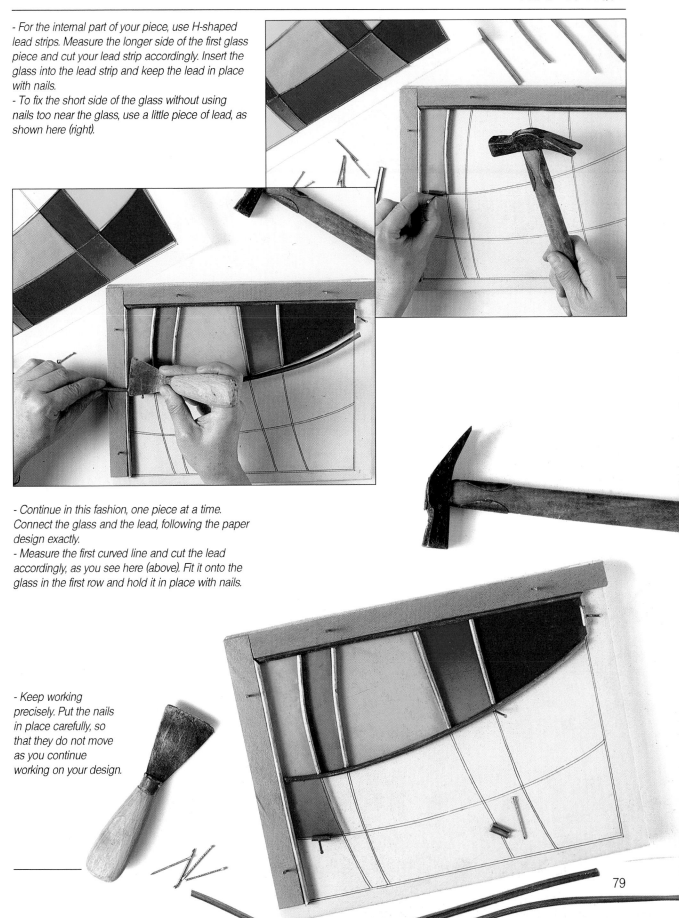

- Continue in this fashion, one piece at a time. Connect the glass and the lead, following the paper design exactly.
- Measure the first curved line and cut the lead accordingly, as you see here (above). Fit it onto the glass in the first row and hold it in place with nails.

- Keep working precisely. Put the nails in place carefully, so that they do not move as you continue working on your design.

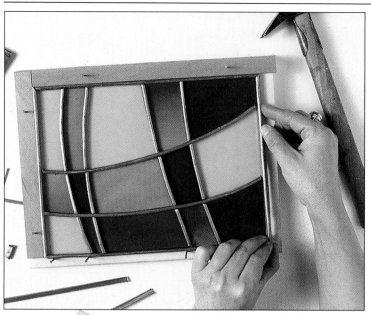

- The glasswork is almost finished. Cut the lead in the proper length and keep your work in place with nails.
- Attach the outside lead strips in order to finish off the work. For the outside edges, use C-shaped lead wire. Measure carefully and cut the wire with the cutter. Insert the glass into the lead, keeping your work in place with the nails.

- Now you can weld the piece. First, weld the joints where the lead strips intersect. Do not weld lead for too long, because it is easy to break. The welder to the right has a thermostat that maintains a constant temperature. The flat head is good for soldering lead. The other pointed head is for finishing off.

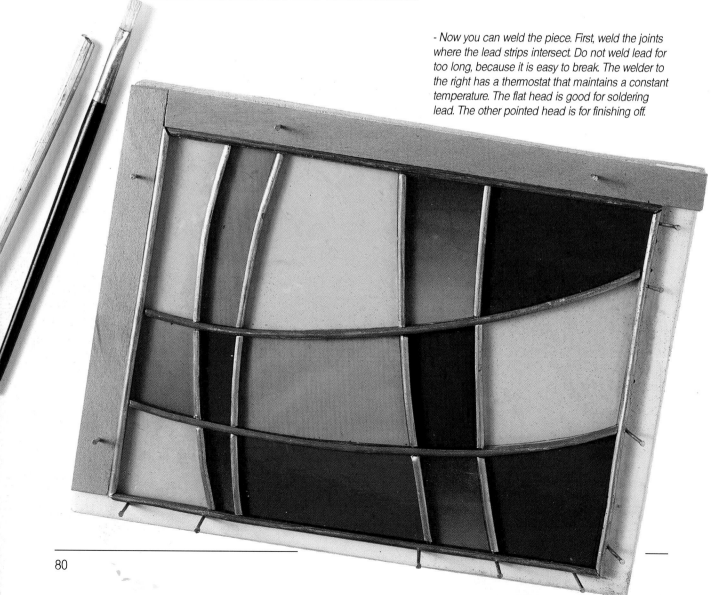

- Cover the welded places with the flux.
- Melt a drop of solder so that it covers the welded intersections. Do this part quickly so that you don't melt the lead.

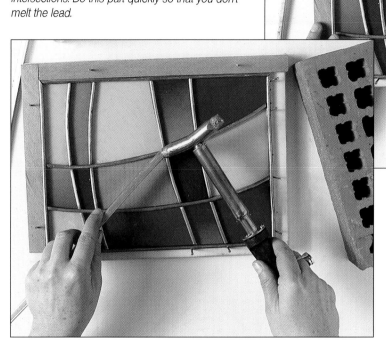

- Weld until you have finished this side. Carefully remove the nails and turn the glasswork over. Repeat these steps on the other side.

SEALING

EQUIPMENT

- plaster, grout, or putty powder
- vinyl glue
- lampblack
- sawdust
- paintbrush
- bristle brush

When the thickness of the glass is less than the grooves in the lead wire, the glass will move, even when it is in the grooves. To prevent any movement, you must seal your glasswork.

- In a bowl, add some plaster powder, a little water, some vinyl glue, and a pinch of lampblack. Mix the ingredients until the texture is creamy. Paint it on the glass with a paintbrush, making sure to fill in the gaps between the glass and lead.

- Let this sit for ten minutes.

- To clean off the glass, you will need some sawdust and a little bristle brush. Cover the glass with the sawdust. Rub the glass well with your hands so that the sawdust absorbs all the excess liquid. The bristle brush will help clean off the piece.

- With the spatula, make sure to clean out all the bits of sawdust and then repeat the process on the other side of the glasswork.

FLOWER TRAY

EQUIPMENT

- wooden frame with clear glass base
- strips of opalescent glass 16 x 12 inches
  (40 x 30 cm) in red, yellow, white, transparent,
  and several greens
- glass cutter
- pliers
- lead wire in C-shape and H-shape
- 50/50 solder
- flux

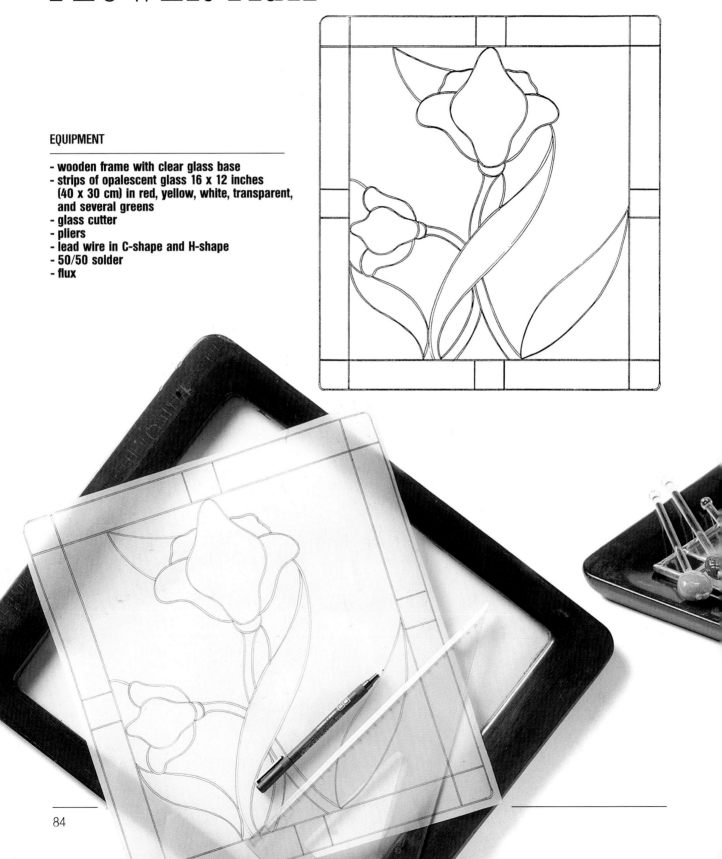

- Practice your design several times with different colors. Then, buy the corresponding glass. Adjust the measurements necessary to make the tray and draw your design. If necessary, use a photocopier to adjust the size. Make one copy on paper and one on cardboard.

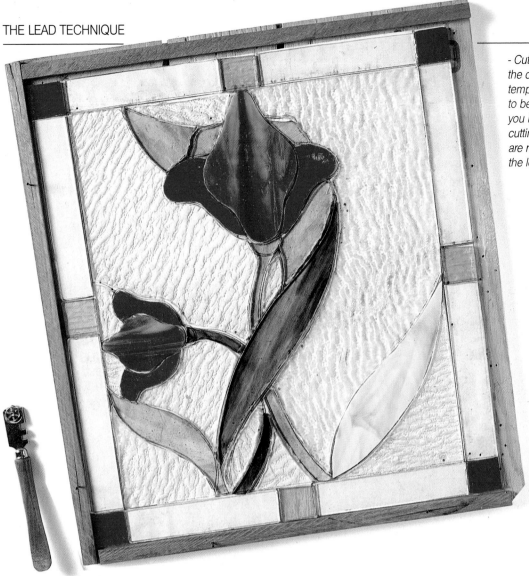

- Cut the glass following the cardboard templates. Remember to be precise. When you have finished cutting the glass, you are ready to trim with the lead wire.

- For the outside edges, use the C-shaped wire. After stretching it out and measuring it, cut it. Place the wire near the wooden band that you have nailed down.
- Insert the first piece of glass – the red square – in the corner. Add a small piece of lead wire and then insert the piece of clear glass. Remember to insert the glass completely into the grooves.

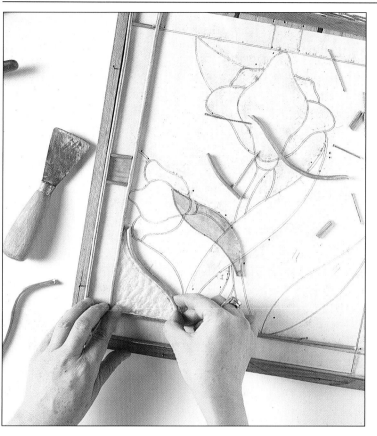

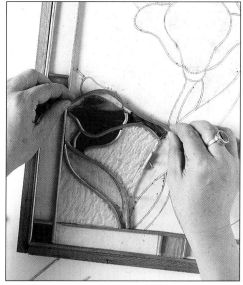

- Here, you are working with H-shaped lead wire. Bend it to fit around the glass pieces that you have cut.
- Before cutting the lead wire, measure how much you will need by matching it to the design.

- Mark the point where you want to cut the lead and use the spatula/cutter to do so.
- Using the spatula, position the wire and hammer when necessary to make sure the wire and glass fit together well. Use nails to keep your work from moving.
- Continue working with one piece of glass at a time. Be sure that you fit the various pieces together accurately.

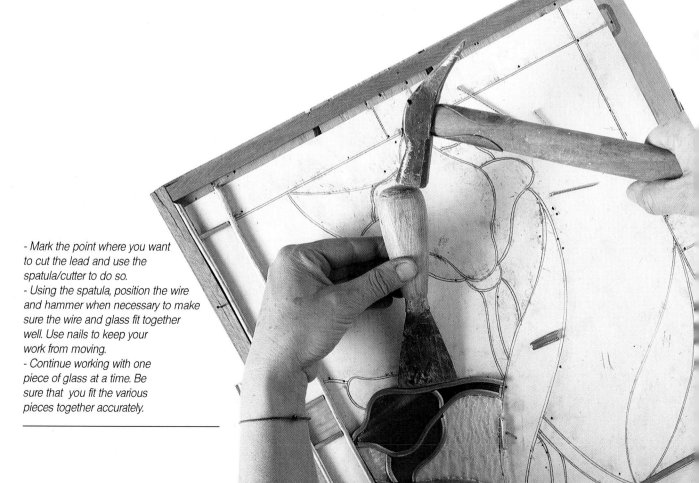

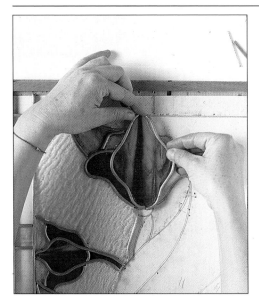

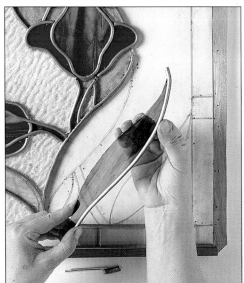

- Cutting the glass pieces and inserting the lead in this project is very difficult, but if you have succeeded with the other projects in this book, you are capable of creating this piece of glasswork.
- Arm yourself with lots of patience and be very accurate, particularly when shaping the lead around the glass pieces.

- Measure the last lead strips and use the spatula to join them to the glass. Push the glass securely into the wire grooves.

- Insert the last pieces of glass into the tray. All the glass pieces should fit exactly, so that your glasswork is an exact replica of your original drawing.
- Use the last strips of C-shaped lead wire as a border for the work. Push the wire grooves onto the glass edges.

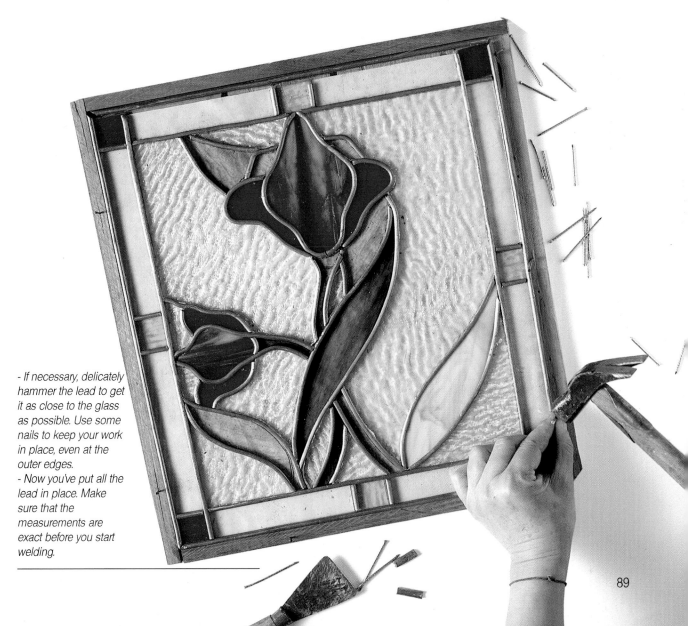

- If necessary, delicately hammer the lead to get it as close to the glass as possible. Use some nails to keep your work in place, even at the outer edges.
- Now you've put all the lead in place. Make sure that the measurements are exact before you start welding.

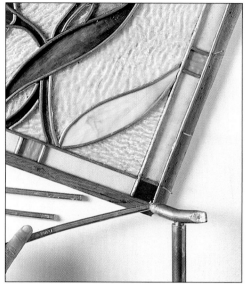

- Use a paintbrush to apply the flux on all the intersections of lead. Begin welding from the outside and remember to drop a touch of solder on the junctures to cover the points where the lead wires cross.

- Weld all the joints. Pause when necessary to add a drop of solder over the welded intersections, making certain not to damage the lead. Continue until you have finished the front.

- *Gently turn the piece over and repeat the welding steps on the back.*

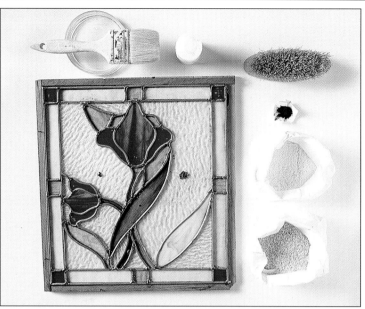

- Prepare to seal your piece with the necessary items: a small bowl, a little water, some plaster powder, vinyl glue, and a pinch of lampblack.

- Mix all the ingredients well. The sealer should have a creamy consistency.
- Use the paintbrush to spread the paste, making sure to get into the spaces between the lead and the glass.

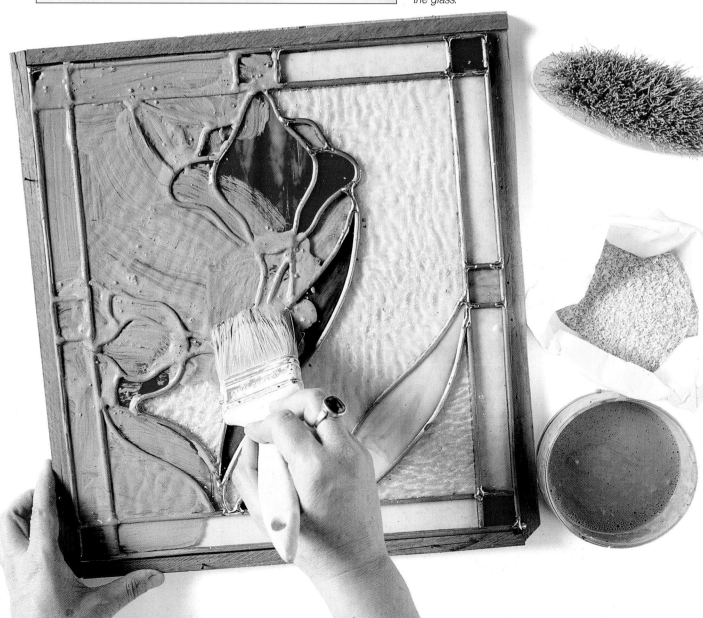

- Let your piece sit for ten minutes and then begin to clean it with sawdust. Rub the piece well with your hands so that the sawdust absorbs the excess sealing paste.
- Use a small brush to wipe the excess away and go over your glasswork with the spatula to eliminate any remaining bits of sawdust. Turn your piece over and finish the other side using the same procedure.

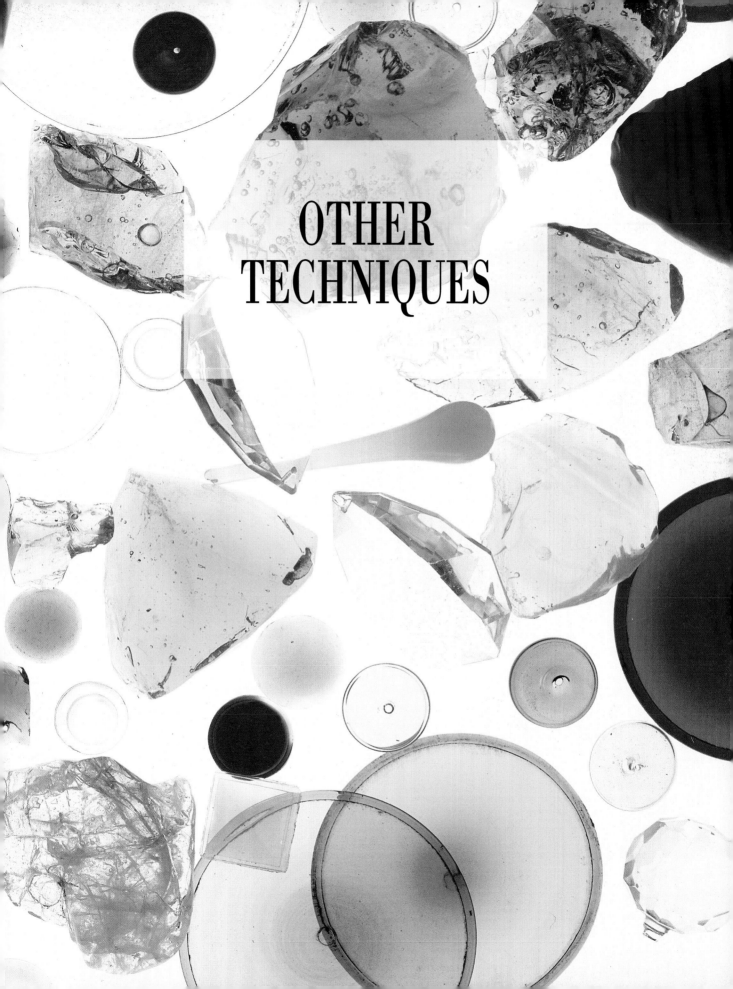

OTHER
TECHNIQUES

FUSED GLASS

COMPATIBLE GLASS

Compatible glass works best for fusion. You can melt the pieces into each other, and, after they cool down, they are similar. The glass has no tension that could cause the final piece to break. In recent years, we've seen an increase in the production of varying types in beautiful colors.

Here, we've created a soap dish and a toothbrush holder from turquoise glass.

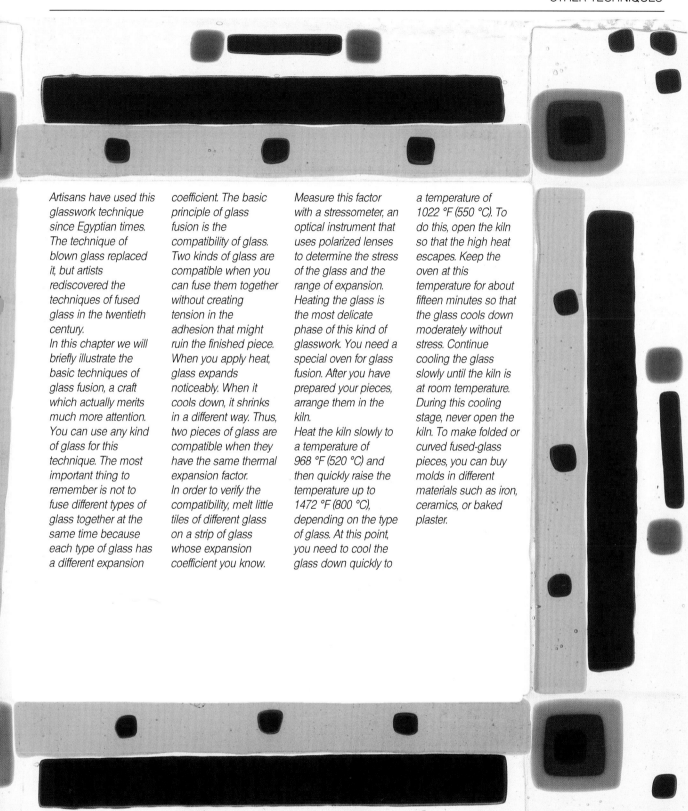

Artisans have used this glasswork technique since Egyptian times. The technique of blown glass replaced it, but artists rediscovered the techniques of fused glass in the twentieth century.

In this chapter we will briefly illustrate the basic techniques of glass fusion, a craft which actually merits much more attention. You can use any kind of glass for this technique. The most important thing to remember is not to fuse different types of glass together at the same time because each type of glass has a different expansion coefficient. The basic principle of glass fusion is the compatibility of glass. Two kinds of glass are compatible when you can fuse them together without creating tension in the adhesion that might ruin the finished piece. When you apply heat, glass expands noticeably. When it cools down, it shrinks in a different way. Thus, two pieces of glass are compatible when they have the same thermal expansion factor.

In order to verify the compatibility, melt little tiles of different glass on a strip of glass whose expansion coefficient you know. Measure this factor with a stressometer, an optical instrument that uses polarized lenses to determine the stress of the glass and the range of expansion. Heating the glass is the most delicate phase of this kind of glasswork. You need a special oven for glass fusion. After you have prepared your pieces, arrange them in the kiln.

Heat the kiln slowly to a temperature of 968 °F (520 °C) and then quickly raise the temperature up to 1472 °F (800 °C), depending on the type of glass. At this point, you need to cool the glass down quickly to a temperature of 1022 °F (550 °C). To do this, open the kiln so that the high heat escapes. Keep the oven at this temperature for about fifteen minutes so that the glass cools down moderately without stress. Continue cooling the glass slowly until the kiln is at room temperature. During this cooling stage, never open the kiln. To make folded or curved fused-glass pieces, you can buy molds in different materials such as iron, ceramics, or baked plaster.

AQUARIUM TABLE

The idea of this piece was to create a watery effect. The table sits on a painted iron base. Placing blue, green, and turquoise glass circles on top of each other produces a sense of the sea. The flying fish accentuate this feeling.

BLUE TRAY

The diameter of this tray is 20 inches (50 cm). The glass was heated and molded on a ceramic fiber base, which produced the wavy effect of the outside border. The splendid cobalt-blue veins in the glass also help create movement in the piece.

STAR PLATE

The star shown here seems to go beyond the edges of the plate.

The contrasting yellow and red make it particularly beautiful.

TRAYS

These transparent rectangular trays with colorful geometric inserts are another example of this versatile glasswork technique.

CHESSBOARDS

These checkerboard or chessboard patterns were made by placing little glass tiles between two sheets of clear glass. Use little glass gems as playing pieces for checkers.

GLASS FUSION PLATES

These are collectible pieces that you can use as a centerpiece or for setting a special table. Create your pattern by placing glass pieces on top of transparent glass. For this plate with red inserts (below), the colored glass was inserted between two pieces of glass, forming a laminated brass layer which oxidizes at high temperatures. This changed its original color.

SMALL SCULPTURES

Using this technique, you can indulge in your fantasies, creating original glass objects.

These pieces have at least five layers of glass, producing a feeling of depth.

CLOCKS

These fused-glass clocks involve a lot of work. Myriad colorful glass pieces were placed on a clear glass base. The result is a decorative and useful glass object.

OTHER SCULPTURES

The fusion of real bottles and glasses becomes a sculpture for your walls.

THE COLLAGE TECHNIQUE

When you design a work using this method, you don't need to draw the double lines that you would when using the Tiffany method or when working with lead wire. Just make single lines. Make the usual two copies on regular paper and on cardboard.

Take a sheet of transparent, unbreakable glass with a minimum thickness of 3/16 inch (5 mm) and the same dimensions as the piece you want to create. Put your paper design under this piece of glass and use your cardboard templates to cut the glass pieces accurately. The cuts should be very precise, because the pieces need to fit together perfectly. Use a grinder if necessary. When you have finished cutting the pieces, place them on the clear glass according to the design underneath. Then remove them all, clean the clear glass thoroughly, and enclose the glass in four pieces of wood that are 1 1/4 inch (3 cm) high. Nail the wood in place. Use a two-part epoxy resin. Mix it well and spread it over the clear glass. The wooden frame will keep the glue from moving. Place all the pieces on the gluey glass base and cover the piece with a thin bead of the resin. Consult the resin instructions for the amount of time required for the glue to harden. After about twelve hours, you can remove the wooden frames and clean your glasswork. Start in a corner and use a straight spatula to help lift up the top layer of resin. This layer should come off like a piece of film. Now your piece is ready to be hung. Use this technique to make large glassworks, as well as the smaller ones you will see in this chapter.

TRAY

This glass-collage base fits inside a thin rectangular iron frame. The precise way the pieces fit together makes this a beautiful piece of glasswork.

COLLAGE TABLE

The table structure is made of burnished iron. The table surface is colored blown glass on a clear, unbreakable glass sheet. This technique allows you to work with large dimensions and big surface areas.

CLOCK

With the collage technique, you can create various kinds of objects, such as this brilliantly colored clock. In order to insert the timing mechanism, you must drill through the clear glass base and then continue with your glass pieces and resin.

IDEAS

I've included this chapter in order to show you how to use the techniques previously described in this book. You'll find ideas to be used as points of departure to make lampshades, mirrors, frames, boxes, and many other objects. With a little creativity and work, you can make a variety of glass objects. Always remember to make the design first and cut the glass very accurately, according to your color pattern. In order to experience good results, you'll need to plan carefully.

SUNFLOWER LAMP

DRAGONFLY LAMP

Flowers work best with opalescent glass, in this case in yellow. We used glass gems for the centers of the flowers and a selection of green glass for the leaves. The base of the lamp is a fused bronze, which imitates the original Tiffany designs.

Tiffany loved dragonflies, and his designs are incredibly creative. In this interpretation, the wings are particularly beautiful. We glued brass mesh to the glass pieces and then attached them to the copper tape, giving the wings their veins. The bronze base also has dragonflies on it, echoing the theme of the lamp.

TABLE LAMP

To create this lamp, use opalescent glass in warm colors and add the section of colored glass stones to create a warm, but vibrant lamp. A solid brass frame, painted black, holds the glass together. The triangle is 20 inches (50 cm) high, and the base is 20 inches (50 cm) long.

With a height of 9 3/4 inches (25 cm), this square-based lamp uses opalescent glass with little glass gems added for whimsy. The same design appears on all sides. It is 9 3/4 inches (25 cm) high. The base is 6 x 6 inches (15 x 15 cm).

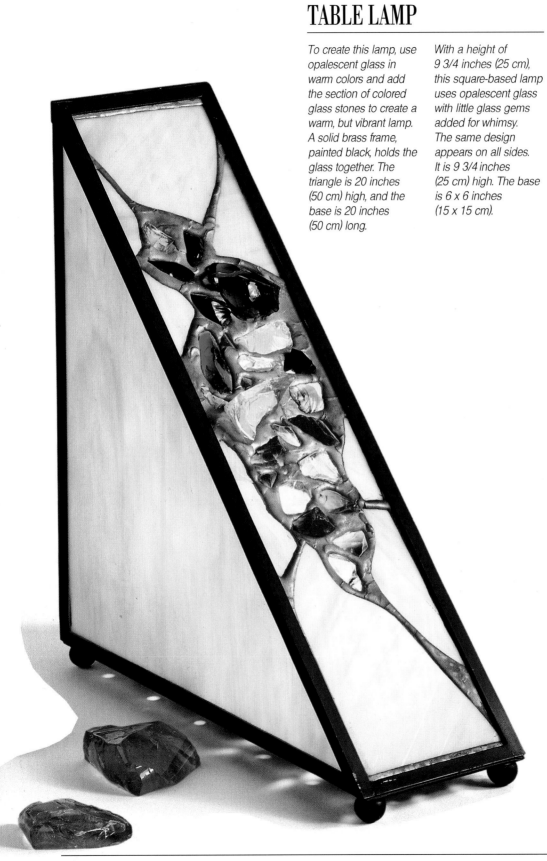

CUBE LAMP

To make this lamp, you need to use opalescent cathedral glass, 12 x 12 inches (30 x 30 cm). Make five copies on paper and five copies on cardboard for each side. Cut the glass. Weld the pieces of glass together, leaving a little space so that the heat of the light bulb can escape. Then, weld the sides together at 90° angles. On the inside, weld two brass rods to attach the light-bulb holder.

SMALL CUBE LAMP

Made with the same procedure as above, this little lamp measures 6 x 6 inches (15 x 15 cm). It is different because you cut the glass in circles or semicircles. Here, too, you leave little spaces between the glass pieces to allow the heat of the light bulb to escape.

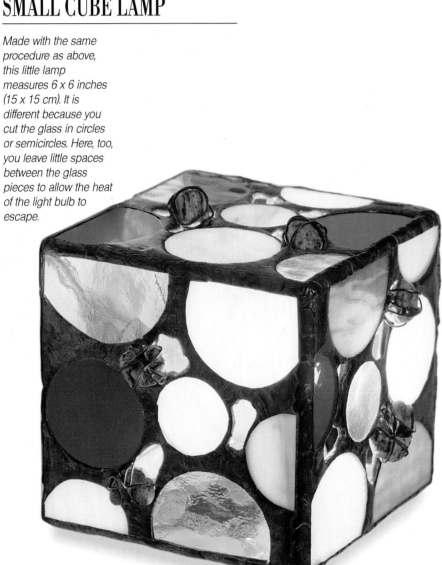

DRAGONFLY LAMP

This lamp is shaped like a pyramid. The stylized dragonflies appear on opposite corners and are made of Venetian gray, orange, and yellow glass. The background is a white opalescent glass.

CORNER LAMP

Use a triangular base for this pretty lamp created with a bellflower and leaf design. The cobalt color of some of the flowers brightens up the muted rose and green tones of the glass.

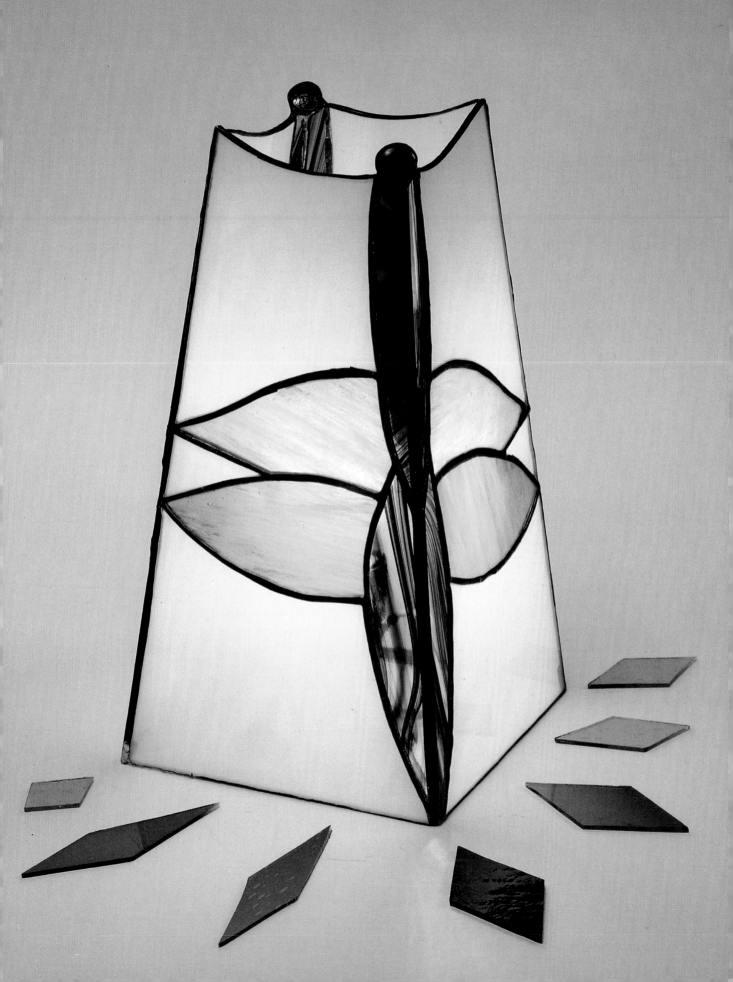

SMALL GLASS HANGINGS

These hang at a window on a small chain. They are a tradition in northern Europe. As the light goes through the glass, it creates a lovely effect.

This water lily, which I made twenty years ago, is one of my favorite flowers.

BUTTERFLY

This butterfly belongs to a series of my window hangings. Before welding the borders, cut the glass accurately according to your design. You can see that the colors include both stained glass and opalescent glass in a range of blues and greens.

MODERN GLASS

Here are two pieces of glasswork from the modern period, made using cathedral glass and lead. They were part of a single window that had six panes, each with a different design.

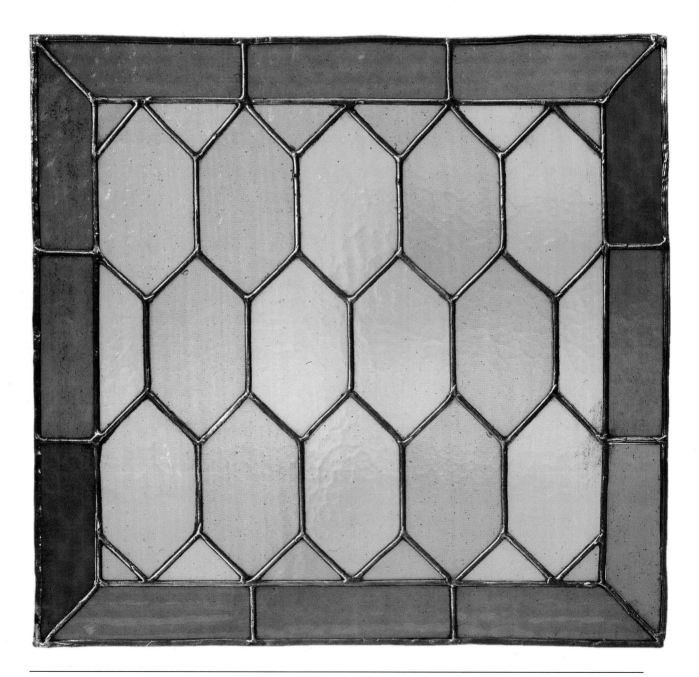

ART DECO MIRRORS

These mirrors are 24 inches (60 cm) in diameter. They stand on iron bases high enough to allow them to be placed near a good light source so that the glass shines on the mirror. Each mirror shape is different, and the borders have a linear design interspersed with waves of different color. Both use stained glass and opalescent glass.

BOXES

The Tiffany technique lends itself beautifully to making these little objects. You can create boxes in various shapes, or you can get ideas from the examples shown here.

To liven up your creations, you can add other elements to the glass surface. In this case, shells from a beach vacation add to the originality of the piece.

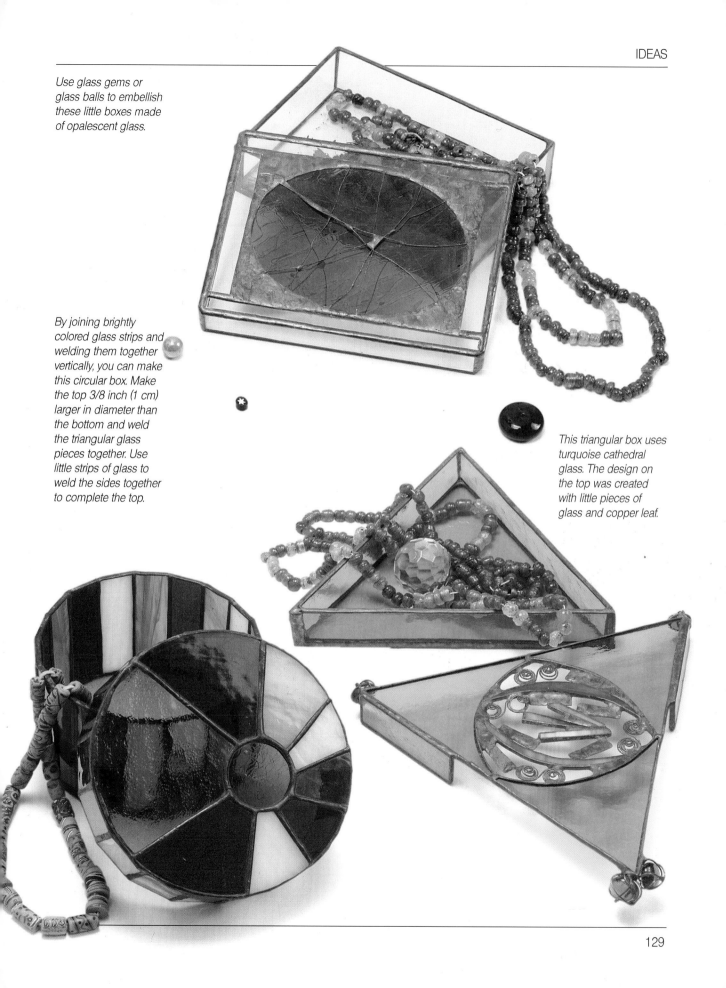

Use glass gems or glass balls to embellish these little boxes made of opalescent glass.

By joining brightly colored glass strips and welding them together vertically, you can make this circular box. Make the top 3/8 inch (1 cm) larger in diameter than the bottom and weld the triangular glass pieces together. Use little strips of glass to weld the sides together to complete the top.

This triangular box uses turquoise cathedral glass. The design on the top was created with little pieces of glass and copper leaf.

RED CONTAINERS

Here's a desk set made with various pieces of glass cut in harlequin style welded to a clear glass base and finished with a drop of melted solder. The objects here are a wastepaper basket, a pen holder, and a paper-clip holder.

OTHER CONTAINERS

We created these bowls in a range of blues and greens, using some yellow as well. Before making your bowl, decide on the angle you want for the sides. You can make the bowl more open or more perpendicular depending on your ideas. The pen holder has a triangular base, and one of the three sides has a star motif.

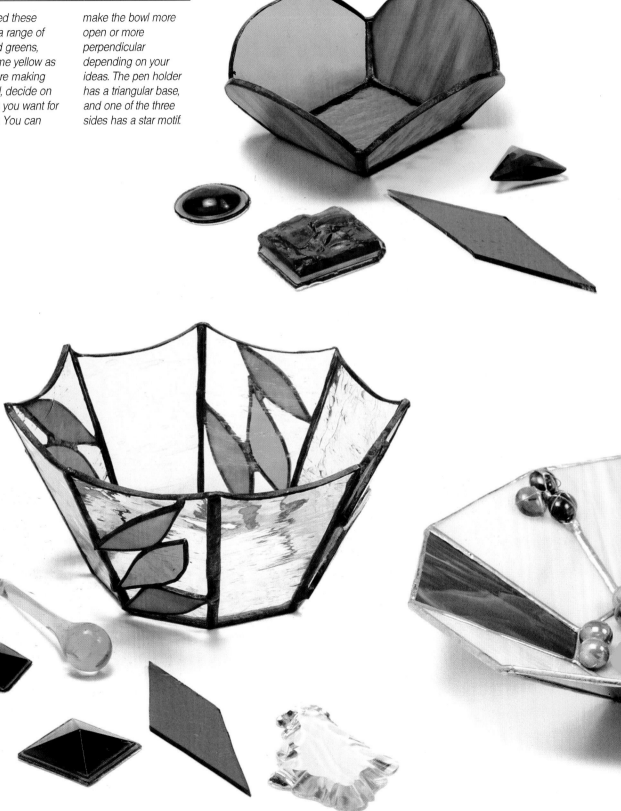

CANDLE HOLDERS

You can make candle holders in the shape of a flower or a star using an infinite number of color combinations for the glass and for the candles themselves.

BOTTLE TOPS

These bottle tops are an original idea. Weld different pieces of glass on a circular base of glass with a diameter of 1 1/4 inch (3 cm). You can also use glass balls, beads, gems, and other decorative elements. Glue a cork to the base and use them on your favorite bottles.

FROM ART
TO ARTWORK

I am ending this book with the work I have done since 1979. I hope to communicate my passion for the art of glasswork, and I hope that my efforts to explain the techniques have been helpful.

In this chapter, I also want to show you the work of an artist / craftsman whom I highly respect.
Giuseppe Codena is an excellent painter who makes his pieces by painting the glass,

heating it in a hot oven, and then binding it with the lead technique. He has worked with well-known painters, following their designs, and he has created glasswork for churches. Some of his work is in Japan.

CROCODRAGON

The design on this three-panel screen represents an imaginary animal swimming in the waves of a rough sea. The animal is in deep green. The crest on his back is a vibrant orange. Various shades of blue create the stormy sea. The frame of the screen is iron, painted black.

FROM AN ARTIST'S SKETCH

This panel (right) measures 98 1/2 x 71 inches (250 x 180 cm). To make it, I used flashy colors of blown glass that I treated with grisaille to obtain a cloudy effect. In addition, I added some parts using the glass-fusion technique. This is one of the few pieces that I have created using someone else's design. I have a lot of respect for the artist Ignazio Moncada. We worked very well together, and we were both very pleased with the result.

REVOLVING DOOR

A SOLUTION FOR YOUR BATHROOM

This luminous glass piece, mounted in an iron frame, serves as a revolving door. In addition to the blown stained glass, we added mosaic glass tiles.

This piece has an aluminum support structure. We used various shades of white glass with a sprinkling of blue, green, and purple shapes. Its proximity to the mirror enhances and reflects it.

ART DECO DOOR

The geometric design of these sliding doors uses eleven kinds of white, transparent, iridescent, stained, and opalescent glass to exploit an incredible variety of light. The result produces the effect of lace.

ARAB-STYLE GLASSWORK

This panel measures 73 x 48 1/2 inches (185 x 123 cm). We used blown glass with mother-of-pearl inserts. The design is typical of Arab inlays used for furniture, and the geometric nature lends itself easily to glasswork. The mother-of-pearl glass is 1/8 inch (3 mm) thick and produces the luminosity of opalescent glass.

BOW WINDOW

The architect Alessandro Mendini collaborated on the creation of this window pane (right), one of six panes looking out on a magnificent garden. The design has only simple color elements so as not to reduce the incoming light.

OVAL

The beautifully formed oval glasswork separates a bathroom from nearby storage space. In addition to the special decorative effect it gives to the house, it provides the only light source for the dark storage room. In order to maintain the privacy of the bathroom, we did not use transparent glass.

LARGE GLASSWORKS

This glasswork wall replaced a real wall in order to create a hallway. Its dimensions are 13 x 13 feet (4 x 4 m), including the door. The design is a seascape with rocks, shells, dolphins, sea horses, and a large jellyfish. For the underwater background, we used blown-bottle glass. The dolphins are iridescent, and they generate a different light than the background. When appropriately lit, this wall is a good source of light for the bedroom next door.

ARC

This piece stands over the doorway of a café. The base is 79 inches (200 cm). We placed uneven pieces of glass at random on a dark gray blown-glass base. Then we welded the whole together with colored glass stones.

AN ARTIST'S WORK

Giuseppe Codena lives and works in Milan and has taught glass techniques to students in secondary education for many years. In particular, he has taught the old grisaille techniques of painting glass and baking enamels at high temperatures. These techniques are over 1,000 years old. Using glass, he has reproduced paintings by the great masters, and he has created glassworks for the cathedral of Monza and the church of San Carlo in Milan. Some of his works are in Japan, including the Fukuoka subway.

HORSE

Count Guido Guidi, who is passionate about horses, commissioned this piece. Codena used the same techniques as for the previous piece. It measures 24 x 32 inches (60 x 80 cm).

PAN PLAYS HIS FLUTE

Created for a splendid villa in Marrakech, this piece uses blown glass painted with brown, red, and black grisaille and painted overlays baked in a hot oven. Codena welded the entire piece together using the lead technique.

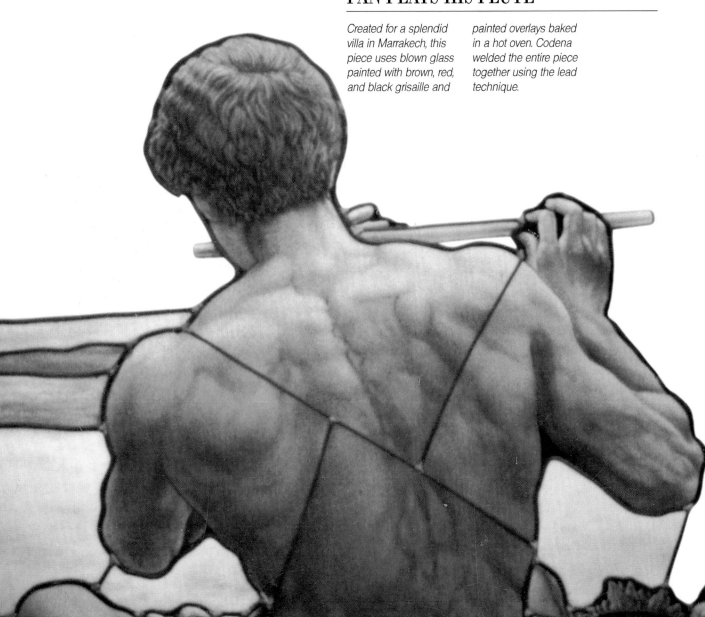

GLASSWORK DESIGNS

On the following pages, you will find various ideas for glasswork. After photocopying the designs and enlarging them to the dimensions you need, you should then test out color variations by trying different combinations on your paper design. The suggestions here are geometric and easy to cut, but I have also included Liberty-style flower designs, which are more difficult to cut.

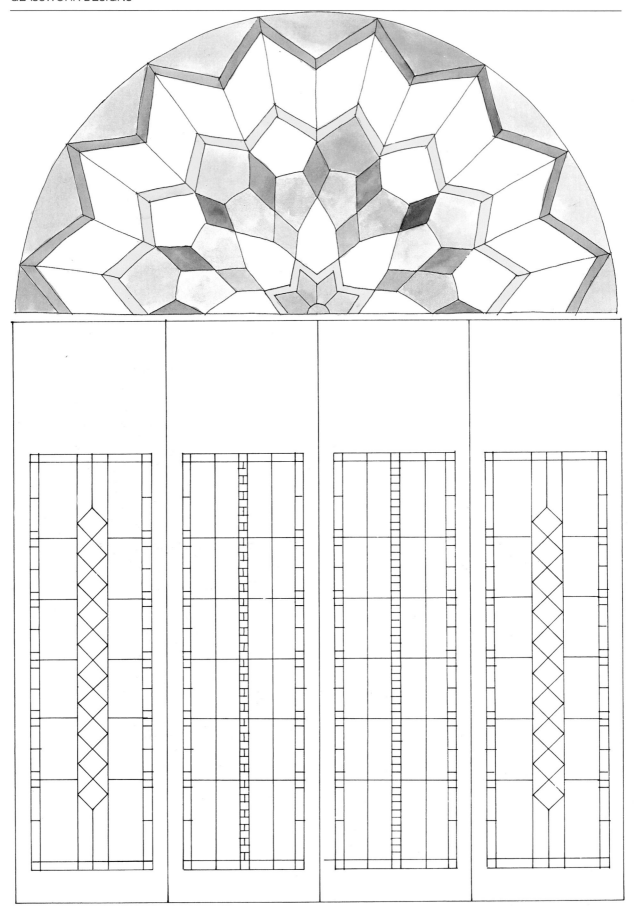

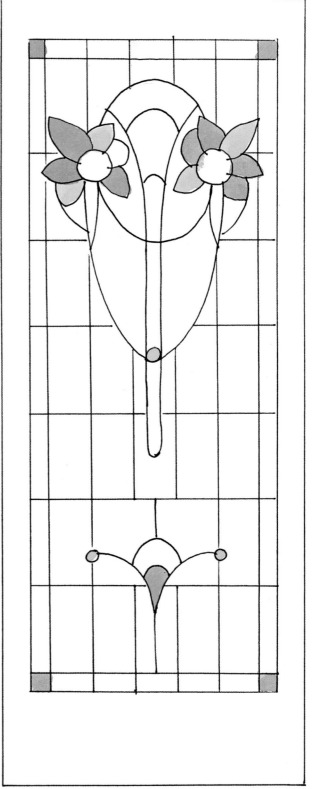

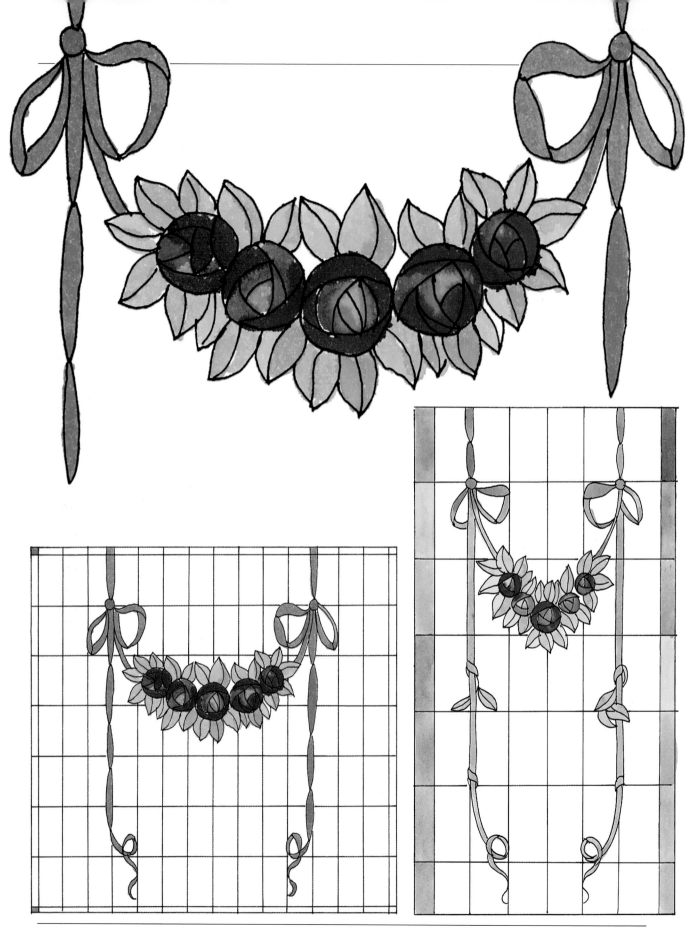

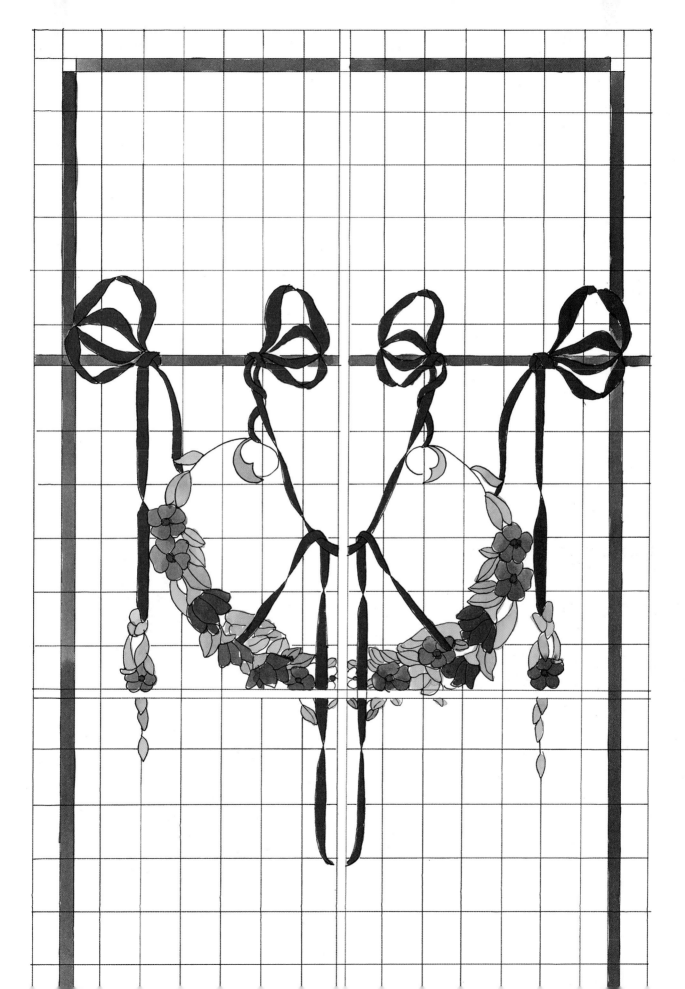